Meatless Cooking
the Natural Way

Meatless Cooking the Natural Way

Robert W. Pelton

South Brunswick and New York: A. S. Barnes and Company
London: Thomas Yoseloff Ltd

A. S. Barnes and Co., Inc.
Cranbury, New Jersey 08512

Thomas Yoseloff Ltd
108 New Bond Street
London W1Y OQX, England

Library of Congress Cataloging in Publication Data

Pelton, Robert W   1934–
    Meatless cooking the natural way.

    1. Vegetarianism.   2. Cookery, American.
I. Title.
TX837.P45   1974   641.5′636   73-111
ISBN 0-498-01275-1

PRINTED IN THE UNITED STATES OF AMERICA

Dedicated to

some of the earlier members of my family —the Peltons, Mitchells, Collisters, Northrups, Daniels, and Tylers;

and especially to

Barnabus Horton of Leichestershire, England, who came to America on the ship *Swallow* some time between 1633 and 1638 with his wife Mary and two children, Joseph and Benjamin. They landed at Hampton, Massachusetts, and were Puritans;

and also to

my great-great-grandmother Huldah (Radike) Horton, one of the finest and most famous horsewomen of her day. She rode with Lafayette in a parade in his honor in Newburgh, New York, in 1824. The French general and friend of the young country was making his second and last visit.

And God said, Behold, I have given you every herb bearing seed, which is upon the face of all the earth, in which is the fruit of a tree yielding seed; to you it shall be for meat. And to every beast of the earth, and to every fowl of the air, and to every thing that creepeth upon the earth, wherein there is life, I have given every green herb for meat: and it was so.

—Genesis

Contents

7

Preface

Meatless Cooking the Natural Way offers the modern home-maker a unique collection of tasty recipes that really are different. These special and tantalizing natural food cookery ideas are presented to assist today's housewife (or singles) in arranging delectable menus.

Tastes vary greatly. Therefore, an appetizing variety of healthful natural food recipes have been included. They have been selected for their overall eye appeal, aroma, ease of digestion, and flavor.

No recipe is really very time consuming—especially when the end result is considered. Nor are any of these natural food recipes expensive or even complicated to properly prepare. Common dishes with which everyone is familiar have been excluded.

In a short time it will become relatively simple to plan a well-balanced and completely nutritious meal with only natural ingredients. And all of this is easily accomplished without the use of meat in any form. Such table offerings are extremely tasty. They satisfy the heartiest appetite. Great variety, exciting colors, and nutrition are the main considerations.

Meat of some sort is the customary highlight of most ordinary meals served in the average American home today.

9

Arranging natural food, meatless menus, is not at all difficult. Wonderful meat substitutes are thoroughly covered
herein. These tasty recipes and suggestions will overcome
the lack of meat on the table. Each will help in contribut-
ing to better health and the well-being of all people.

Every recipe included in this book was a popular favorite in the long-forgotten past. Many were coveted within
a family and handed down over numerous generations.
Others are historical gems, for they were inventions of, or
favorites of, some notable family of long ago. Each is appetizing as well as nutritious—and concocted only with natural and unadulterated ingredients.

Some Useful American, English and Metric Equivalent Measures

U. S. *Liquid Measures*	*Metric*
1 gallon	3.785 liters
1 quart	.946 liters
1 fluid ounce	29.573 mililiters

U. S. *Dry Measures*	*Metric*
1 quart	1.101 liters
1 pint	.550 liters
1 teaspoon	4.9 cubic centimeters
1 tablespoon	14.8 cubic centimeters
1 cup	236.6 cubic centimeters

U. S.	*English*
1.032 dry quarts	1 quart
1.201 liquid quarts	1 quart
1.201 gallons	1 gallon

1 English pint	20 fluid ounces
1 American pint	16 fluid ounces
1 American cup	8 fluid ounces
8 American tablespoons	4 fluid ounces
1 American tablespoon	½ fluid ounce
3 American teaspoons	½ fluid ounce
1 English tablespoon	⅔ to 1 fluid ounce (approx.)
1 English tablespoon	4 teaspoons

The American measuring tablespoon holds ¼ oz. flour

11

Meatless Cooking
the Natural Way

1

Using Herbs
in Preparing Natural Foods

The word herb is generally used in a rather broad sense. It denotes anything of a vegetable origin used to impart a special aromatic flavor or pleasing odor to a fantastic variety of foods.

More specifically, the word *herb* includes aromatic leaves, stalks, or flowers of a particular plant. It may even be the oil from a plant, the root of a plant, or the entire plant itself. Seeds are also classed in the herbal realm. They too are aromatic and are added to food in their dry form. A seed may sometimes be an entire fruit of a plant, or merely a *seed* as the name implies.

The careful application of such items in natural cooking will always enhance rather than hide or overpower the delightful natural flavor of any particular recipe dish. Adding herbs properly to any kind of natural food will add a great deal of excitement to many otherwise ordinary-tasting dishes. Delectable culinary results can easily be obtained when herbs are used in the correct manner.

Individual tastes differ. The secret of herb cookery is to

15

use these aromatic ingredients sparingly and to personal taste. Always use too little rather than too much. More can always be added when necessary.

Careful experimentation is the key to successful herb cookery. Each meal can be made into an adventure of new and unusual taste. Herbs allow anyone to serve meals that are more appetizing, tastier, and more pleasing to the smell. They contain a rich supply of natural vitamins. And they make foods more readily digestable.

Herb cookery does not have to be any more expensive than ordinary meal preparation. Nor does it have to take more time. The alphabetical list below consists of those herbs which are presently popular in natural food cookery. And each is readily available in its pure, untainted form.

Popular Herbal Cooking Aids

ALLSPICE (*Pimenta officinalis*): A berry of the evergreen tree that is related to the myrtle family. Commonly used in whole berry form in roasts, soup, stews, pickles, etc. Used ground in cakes, fruit pies, cookies, roasts, meat loafs, soups, catsup, sauces, candies, etc. Tastes similar to a mixture of cinnamon, cloves, and nutmeg. Its flavor intensifies when food is allowed to stand. This is the only major spice exclusively produced in the western hemisphere.

ANISE (*Pimpinella anisum*): The seed of a plant related to the parsley family. The oil (extract) of this grey-green seed is used in certain types candies, pastries, and breads. The seed is used either whole or ground in stews, fish, pickles, salad dressings, cookies, candy, cakes, bread, etc. The taste is similar to that of licorice. Anise is imported from Mexico and areas of the Mediterranean.

BALM (*Balsamon*): The leaves of this herb are used in many soups, dressings, sauces, and desserts. Also used to garnish iced tea, fruit drinks, and punches.

BASIL (*Ocimum basilicum*): The leaf of a plant related to the mint family. Commonly used as a dried leaf in soups, fish dishes, meat loaf, cheese dishes, spaghetti sauce, tomato dishes, salad dressings, stuffings, stews, etc. Smells much like cloves. Usually imported from India and northern Mediterranean countries.

BAY LEAVES (*Laurus nobilis*): The dried green leaves of the evergreen tree. This dried leaf is used in fish dishes, pickling solutions, any tomato dish, soups, salad dressings, cooking most vegetables, roasts, stews, etc. It has an almost bitter flavor and a strong pungent smell. The flavor of bay leaves intensifies in relation to how long the food is cooked. Usually imported from areas in the Mediterranean.

BOUQUET GARNI: Made by tying thyme, bay leaves, and parsley in a coarse muslin (or cheesecloth) bag. Cooked in all varieties of dishes. Various other herbs can be added as desired. The bouquet garni bag is to be removed before the food is served.

CARAWAY SEEDS (*Carum carvi*): A small brown seed from a plant related to the parsley family. Used in rye bread, corn bread, cookies, stews, soups, salads, all meats, pastries, *canapés* fillings, hors d'oeuvres, etc. Improves the taste of many natural foods because of its pleasant, rather sweet flavor. To be used rather sparingly in every case. Generally imported from the Netherlands.

CARDAMOM (*Elletaria cardamomum*): A small, three-sided aromatic seed from a plant related to the ginger family. It is commonly used in ground form in Danish pastries, muffins, fruit dishes, coffeecakes, sweet breads, etc. Used whole in roasts, hot wines, punches, with fruit dishes, pickles, etc. Has a sweet flavor. Should always be used with discretion. Imported from Ceylon, Guatemala, and India.

CASSIA: *See* Cinnamon.

CELERY (*Apium graveolens*): Celery seed is the dried seed from a celery plant. It is commonly used in pickling solutions, breads, tomato dishes, pastries, meat loaf, salad dressings, soups, salads, relishes etc. Celery seeds are aromatic and have a slightly bitter taste. They smell like celery. These seeds are imported from France and India. Celery flakes are made from dried leaves and stalks of the American celery plant. They are used for seasoning in vegetable juice cocktails, stews, salads, soups, roasts, fowl, etc. Often used as a garnish on various dishes.

CHERVIL: A common substitute for parsley, but with a much more delicate flavor. Commonly used as a garnish for salads, or as a seasoning for soups and sauces.

CHIVES (*Cepa*): A plant of the onion family. The leaves are finely chopped up for use in stews, salads, omelets, soups, cheese dishes, etc. It has a mild, onionlike flavor. Chives are also used as a garnish on baked potatoes, etc.

CINNAMON (*Cinnamomum zeylanicum*): Comes from the inner bark of an evergreen that is related to the laurel family. Whole cinnamon (sticks) is used in stewed fruits, numerous cooked vegetable dishes, pickling, beverages, etc. Ground cinnamon is used for pies, cooking meats, sweet breads, punches, etc. And it is used for sprinkling on French toast, rolls, custards, doughnuts, etc. Cinnamon is the one most important spice used in baking. It has a sweet, natural flavor and is spicy. This herb is imported from Indonesia and parts of Southeast Asia.

CLOVES (*Eugenia caryophyllata*): The dried, unopened bud taken from the evergreen tree. Related to the myrtle family. This reddish-brown bud is shaped much like a nail. It is commonly used whole as a garnish for glazed meats, roasts, etc. Also used whole to flavor soups, pickles, sauces, etc. Ground cloves are used in cakes, puddings, pickling, vegetable cooking, soups, etc. The sweet pungent flavor intensifies when food is allowed to stand. Always use sparingly. Cloves are imported from the Malagasy Republic, Zanzibar, and the Molucca Islands.

COMINO: *See* Cumin.

CORIANDER: (*Coriandrum sativum*): A dried, lemon-flavored seed from a plant related to the parsley family. Commonly used whole in pickling, biscuits, punches, green salads, meat marinades, and demitasse coffee. Crushed or ground coriander is popularly used in candy, cookies, sweet breads, pastry, fish dishes, fowl, meats, pies, puddings, meat sauces, etc. It is imported from the Mediterranean area and Southern Europe.

CUMIN (*Cuminum cyminum*): The dried seed from a plant related to the parsley family. This yellowish-brown seed is used whole or ground in cheese dishes, soups, pastries, rice dishes, hors d'oeuvres, chili, salad dressings, etc. It is sometimes used as a substitute for *caraway seeds*. This is a very powerful herb and should be used with caution. It has a strong and earthy flavor. Cumin is imported from Morocco and Iran.

CUMMIN: *See* Cumin.

CURRY: A blend of about sixteen different herbs. It is used to add flavor to cream soups, tomato dishes, casseroles, all vegetables, meats, fish, fowl, salad dressings, etc. Should be used sparingly as it may tend to dominate the natural food flavor.

DILL (*Anethum graveolens*): The pungent, light brown, dried seed from a plant related to the parsley family. Used in dill pickles, and to make soups more appetizing, cheese dishes, fish, fowl, salad dressings, etc. Dill seeds are usually imported from India. Fresh dill leaves are finely chopped up and used to complement cream sauces, vegetable salads, salad dressings, egg dishes, vegetables, tomato juice, noodles, rice dishes, cheese dishes, etc. And the leaves are commonly used as a garnish for many dishes. They come from the California dill weed. These leaves are bright green and much more delicately flavored than are the imported seeds.

FENNEL (*Foeniculum vulgare*): The aromatic, yellowish-brown, dried seed from a plant related to the parsley family. These seeds are usually used in pickles, cookies, pies, pastries, salad dressings, vegetable dishes, fish, cakes, etc. Fresh fennel leaves are chopped up and used in many sauces. Its flavor is somewhat like that of licorice. This herb is usually imported from India.

GARLIC (*Allium sativum*): A strong-flavored, extremely popular seasoning. The garlic bulb is related to the lily family. It can be used fresh, or obtained in pure powder form, as a juice, or in chips. Garlic is used in soups, gravies, salad dressings, salads, pickles, meats, fish, fowl, stews, etc. This plant is grown all over the world, and is one of the most popular of all herbal seasonings.

GINGER (*Zingiber officinale*): The sweet, rather hot-flavored, peeled and dried roots of the ginger plant. Whole ginger is used in making pickles, stewing fruit, tea, sauces, etc. Ground ginger is commonly used in cakes, cookies, puddings, meats, soups, all vegetables, etc. It is considered to be one of the most versatile herbs. Fresh ginger root cooked in syrup is a fine-tasting candy. This root is usually imported from Jamaica.

HORSERADISH: An extremely popular ingredient for use in various sauces, salads, pickling solutions, meats, *canapé* spreads, etc.

HYSSOP: The leaves and flowers of this plant are commonly used to flavor soups, salads, beverages, and candies.

JAMAICA PEPPER: *See* Allspice.

JAMAICA PIMENTO: *See* Allspice.

LAUREL LEAVES: *See* Bay leaves.

LEMON PEEL (*Citrus limon*): The dried rind of the fresh lemon. Used to flavor frostings, cakes, cookies, breads, puddings, pies, fowl, meat sauces, stuffings, vegetables, etc. Grated fresh lemon rinds or peels are more flavorful than are the dried type. And they are more nutritious.

MACE (*Myristica fragrans*): Comes from the dried skin that covers the *nutmeg*. It is the covering from the fruit of a tree related to the evergreen family. Mace is bright red when fresh, and when dried, appears to be a brown-orange color. It is commonly used as a substitute for *nutmeg* in many recipes but this herb is much milder. Used with most vegetable dishes, cakes, frostings, puddings, soups, meats, fish, creamed dishes, pastries, etc. Mace is imported from the West Indies and Indonesia.

MARJORAM (*Majorana hortensis*): A rather bitter but pleasant-flavored leaf from a plant related to the mint family. It is grey-green in color. Marjoram can be used in the ground form or as dried leaves. It is used sparingly on meats, fowl, fish, green salads, etc. This herb blends well with cheese dishes, and with other herbs for soups, sauces, and salad dressings. It enlivens the flavor of most vegetables such as peas, lima beans, potatoes, etc.

MINT (*Mentha spicata*): The aromatic, sweet-flavored leaf of the spearmint plant. Used dried or fresh in flake form, or as an extract. The fresh leaves are excellent as a garnish for many types of food and beverages. Fresh or dried mint is used for making teas, punches, soups, jellies, candies, and fruit dishes. Finely chopped mint leaves are a delight when sprinkled over peas and carrots just before they are served on the table.

MUSTARD (*Brassica hirta* or *Brassica juncea*): An annual herb that primarily grows in Montana and California. Bears a small, pungent-flavored seed. Mustard seeds are used whole in pickling, relishes, corn beef, boiled cabbage, etc. The green, young leaves are commonly used for salads and as a flavorful cooked green. Ground or powdered dry mustard adds unsuspecting flavor to cheese dishes, soups, salad dressings, meats, vegetables, etc.

NUTMEG (*Myristica fragrans*): The dried seed taken from the fruit of a tree related to the evergreen family. It is sweet, spicy, and somewhat warm to the taste. Nutmeg can be used whole or ground. A favorite herb for bringing out the flavor of poultry, fish, meats, vegetables, etc. It can also be sprinkled over sauces, hot and cold drinks, and used in making cakes, pies, etc. Nutmeg is usually imported from the West Indies and Indonesia.

ONION (*Allium cepa*): The onion is one of the most popular natural food flavorings. This plant is related to the lily family. Onion juice and dried onion flakes usually come from the bulb of the plant. Onion flakes or shredded onion are also obtained from the green plant top. This herb is used in almost every imaginable type of natural dish.

ORANGE PEEL (*Citrus sinenis*): The dried rind of the fresh orange. Used to flavor frostings, cakes, cookies, breads, puddings, pies, fowl, meat sauces, stuffings, vegetables, etc. Grated fresh orange rinds or peels are more flavorful than are the dried type. And they are more nutritious.

OREGANO (*Lippia* or *Origanum*): A strong-flavored, aromatic, dried leaf from a perennial plant. It is similar in taste to the *marjoram*. Comes both in leaf form or ground. Generally used to flavor such foods as chili, vegetable soups, tomato dishes, barbecue sauces, cheese dishes, salads, stuffings, and meat sauces.

PAPRIKA (*Capsicum annuum*): A bright red pod taken from a sweet red pepper. It is mild, sweet flavored, and pleasant smelling. Used as an extremely popular ground seasoning for salad dressings, soups, fish, meats, etc. It is a tasty and colorful garnish for egg dishes, salads, etc. Paprika is grown in California as well as imported from Central European countries and Spain.

PARSLEY (*Petroselinum crispum*): The pleasant, mild-smelling, dried curly leaves taken from a biennial plant. It has a rather mild taste and imparts a delicate flavor to soups, sauces, stews, stuffings, salad dressings, fish, meats, and poultry. Primarily used as either a popular flavoring ingredient in food or a garnish on food. It blends extremely well with all other herbs. Parsley is mainly grown in California.

PEPPER (*Piper nigrum*): Black pepper is the dried un-ripe berry of a climbing vine. It is the one most popular herbal spice in the world. White pepper is the inner kernel of the ripe pepper berry. Both are hot and biting to the taste. The white variety is slightly milder than is the black. The black pepper is used whole (peppercorns) in salad dressings, pickling solutions, soups, etc. Ground black pepper is used in every type of dish except something sweet. White ground pepper is commonly used where the dark specks of black pepper are not to be seen. Pepper is imported from Borneo, India, Indonesia, and Malaysia.

PEPPER, RED (*Capsicum frutescens*): The deep red fruit of the pepper plant. This type is in no way related to black or white pepper. It has an extremely hot flavor. Chiefly used on meats, fish, soups, cheese dishes, gravy, pickles, poultry, etc. Widely used in Mexican and Italian food preparations.

PIMENTO: *See* ALLSPICE.

POPPY SEED (*Papaver somniferum*): A tiny, slate-blue, kid-ney-shaped seed from a plant of the poppy family. It has a mild, nutty flavor. Used in all types recipes as an ingredient or merely as a tasty garnish. Contains absolutely no narcotic properties. Poppy seeds are especially good with cheese dishes, cookies, breads, cakes, salads, casseroles, etc. It is usually imported from Iran, the Netherlands, and Poland.

ROSEMARY (*Rosmarinus officinalis*): A dried, pine flavored leaf from an evergreen shrub related to the mint family. It is grey-green and fragrant. Resembles tiny pine needles. The ground dry leaves or the chopped fresh leaves add delicious flavor to all vegetables, stuffing, soups, stews, fish dishes, poultry, lamb, pork, beef, etc. It serves as a base for natural herbal soups. Rosemary is often sprinkled over the live coals when meat is being barbecued. It comes from California, North Carolina, and Virginia. And this herb is also imported from France, Portugal, and other countries.

SAFFRON (*Crocus sativus*): The orange-yellow dried stigma of the saffron crocus. It has a bitter but rather pleasant taste. The stigmas are ground and used to both color and flavor foods. It imparts a yellow color to certain candies and vegetables. Saffron is used as a seasoning for chicken dishes, fish, sauces, rice dishes, soups, yeast breads, etc. It is the world's most expensive herbal spice. This herb should be used sparingly or it will ruin the basic food taste. It is usually imported from Spain.

SAGE (*Salvia officinalis*): The grey-green dried leaf of a plant related to the mint family. It is highly aromatic and has a mildly bitter taste. The dried leaves are powdered and used as a seasoning for dressings, stews, tomato dishes, sauces, cheese dishes, poultry, onions, etc. It should be used very sparingly. Sage is usually imported from Yugoslavia.

SAVORY (*Satureja hortensis*): The brown-green leaf of a plant related to the mint family. It is highly aromatic with a pungent flavor. The leaves are ground and used in stuffings, sauces, soups, meat loaf, gravies, stews, cabbage, etc. It is considered to be the perfect seasoning for all members of the pea-bean-lentil family. Savory is often used as a substitute for *sage*.

SESAME SEED (*Sesamum indicum*): The oval-shaped, dried, hulled seed from an annual tropical herb. It is cream-white and slippery with a nutty almondlike flavor. Sesame seeds are sprinkled on *canapés*, cookies, rolls, breads, cakes, soups, vegetables, etc. They are used in candy, cakes, dips, stuffings, etc. An extremely versatile seed. Usually imported from Central America and India.

SPEARMINT: *See* Mint.

SWEET BASIL: *See* Basil.

TARRAGON (*Artemisia dracunculus*): The dark green, extremely aromatic leaves from a perennial shrub. Used as a garnish on many meat dishes. Popular for seasoning vinegar, pickles, salads, dressings, soups, gravies, spinach, sauces, roasts etc. A few fresh, chopped leaves may be added to egg dishes or mushrooms. Should be used very sparingly. Tarragon is usually imported from France but it is also cultivated in some areas of the United States.

THYME (*Thymus vulgaris*): The grey-green leaves of a plant related to the mint family. It is extremely popular and has a pungent flavor. This herb is quite aromatic. The leaves are powdered and may be used in seasoning pickle solutions, in soups, most vegetables, dressings, fish, meats, poultry, etc. Usually imported from France but also grown in some areas of the United States.

TURMERIC (*Curcuma longa*): The golden yellow root of a plant related to the ginger family. It is slightly bitter with a musky smell. This root is dried in the sun and then ground into powder. Turmeric root powder is used to impart yellow coloring to cheese, butter, egg dishes, pickles, condiments, pastries, breads, noodles, etc. It is imported from Haiti India, Jamaica, and Peru.

VANILLA (*Vanilla planifolia*): The long, slender, unripe bean taken from an orchid plant. It is cured and dried to bring out its natural flavor and aroma. Vanilla is used to flavor many sweet types of food such as cakes, bread, custards, eggnog, pies, frostings, etc. It is usually imported from Madagascar, Mexico, Java, Tahiti, etc.

WATERCRESS: These leaves have a delightful peppery taste. They add great zest to vegetable salads. Also used as a garnish, a popular seasoning, and in soups.

WILD MARJORAM: *See* Oregano.

2

Meaningful Main Dishes
with Natural Foods

STUFFED EGGPLANT
FAVORITE OF JEFFERSON DAVIS

2 large eggplants
2 tablespoons onion,
  minced
1 cup celery, chopped
1 cup bread crumbs
1/2 teaspoon pepper
1 teaspoon salt

1/2 teaspoon nutmeg
1 teaspoon parsley
1 cup nutmeats, chopped
1/2 cup butter, melted
2 cups tomatoes, stewed
2 eggs, well beaten
cream to suit

Put the eggplants in a kettle with enough water to cover them. Parboil (partially cook) for 10 minutes. Then slit each eggplant down the side and extract the seeds. Prop open the cuts with a clean stick of wood. Lay them in cold, salted water while preparing the stuffing.

Fry the onion and celery in butter until nicely browned. Blend these with the rest of the ingredients. Add the cream last and use only enough to moisten the mixture well. Fill the cavity of each eggplant with this stuffing. Wind soft thread around them to keep the slit shut. Place on the rack of a roasting pan. Put a little water in the bottom of the pan. Bake in a moderate oven (350 degrees) for 20 to 25 minutes. Baste with butter and water when they begin to cook. Test with a straw when they are tender. Baste well with butter just before removing them from the pan. Lay the eggplants in a dish. Add 3 tablespoons cream to the drippings in the bottom of the roasting pan. Thicken this with a little flour and put in 1 teaspoon parsley. Bring to a quick boil. Pour over the eggplant and serve immediately. *Note*: Varna Davis often prepared this delightful dish for her husband while he was president of the Confederacy in 1861.

OLD-FASHIONED TOMATO-CORNMEAL LOAF

1 clove garlic, halved	1 tablespoon salt
1 large onion, chopped	1 tablespoon chili powder
2 cups hominy, cooked	1 3/4 cups cornmeal
4 cups tomatoes, stewed	2 1/2 cups milk
3 tablespoons olive oil	3 eggs, well beaten
1 tablespoon butter, melted	1 cup ripe olives, halved

Fry the garlic and onion in butter until browned. Stir in the hominy, tomatoes, olive oil, butter, salt, and chili powder. Bring this to a quick boil. Blend the cornmeal and milk in a wooden mixing bowl. Stir this into the frying pan mixture. Let it all simmer for 10 minutes. Stir constantly. Take the pan from the stove and whip in the frothy beaten eggs. Lastly stir in the olives. Pour into a buttered baking dish. Bake in a moderately hot oven (375 degrees) for 1 hour. Serve in the baking dish while hot.

ASPARAGUS AND EGGS

30 asparagus tips, fresh	Salt to suit
	Pepper to suit
1 cup drawn butter gravy[1]	6 eggs
	Butter bits to suit

Put the asparagus tips in a saucepan and cover with water. Bring to a boil and then simmer for 15 minutes. Drain off all the water and add the drawn butter gravy. Bring to a quick boil, season to taste with salt and pepper, and pour into a buttered baking dish. Smooth over the top of the mixture. Now carefully break the eggs over the surface. Sprinkle with tiny bits of butter, salt, and pepper. Put in a moderate oven (350 degrees) and leave until the eggs have set. Then take out of the oven and serve immediately in the baking dish.

or

You may beat the egg yolks to a custard-like consistency. Then beat the egg whites to a stiff froth. Stir them together and season with salt and pepper. Beat in 3 tablespoons of cream or milk. Pour this evenly over the mixture in the baking dish. *Note*: This, according to my great-great-grandmother, is decidedly the better way of the two. But it is somewhat more troublesome to make properly.

SOUTHERN CREAMED EGGS IN THE OLD DAYS

1 tablespoon flour	Salt to taste
1 tablespoon butter	Pepper to taste
1 cup milk, boiling	1/2 teaspoon parsley,
5 eggs, hardboiled and chopped	chopped fine

---

1. Recipe in Chapter 4.

Put the flour and butter in a wooden mixing bowl and rub to a smooth cream. Blend in the boiling milk. Stir the chopped boiled eggs into this. Season with salt, pepper, and parsley. Serve with a garnish of toast cut into small circles and diamonds. Other flavors may be given to this dish by adding mushrooms or catsup.[2]

REAL OLD-TIME BAKED PEANUT STEAK PATTIES

3 1/2 cups bread crumbs, whole wheat	Pinch of pepper
2 cups peanuts, chopped	1/2 teaspoon mace
1 teaspoon salt	1 teaspoon celery salt
	3 eggs, well beaten
	3/4 cup milk

Blend all of the above ingredients in a wooden mixing bowl. Work together well until the mixture is smooth. Set aside for 45 minutes. Then form into 1/2-inch-thick patties. Brush each cake with melted butter. Place them on a buttered baking pan. Bake in a moderate oven (350 degrees) until browned. Serve with any good gravy.[3]

GREEN CORN PUDDING
A FAVORITE OF ETHAN ALLEN

12 large ears corn	Pinch of salt
5 egg yolks, well beaten	4 cups cream
2 tablespoons butter, melted	or
1 tablespoon sugar	4 cups milk
	5 egg whites, stiffly beaten

Grate the corn (raw) from the cobs and put it in a large wooden mixing bowl. Stir in the custardlike egg yolks and

---

2. Recipes in *Natural Cooking the Old Fashioned Way,* by the author.
3. Recipes in Chapter 4.

beat it together *very* hard. Stir in the melted butter, sugar, and salt. Gradually add the cream or milk, beating hard
all the time. Lastly fold in the fluffy beaten egg whites.
Pour into a deep buttered baking dish. Cover the dish and
bake in a moderate oven (350 degrees) for 1 hour. Then
remove the cover and continue baking until finely browned.

Note: This a most delicious main dish when it is properly mixed and baked. Warm up what is left over from dinner for a nourishing breakfast treat. Moisten it with a little warm milk. Stir it in a saucepan until smoking hot. You
can make this same pudding with home-canned corn during the winter months. Green corn pudding was extremely
popular in the Colonies before the American Revolution. It
was a favorite of Ethan Allen (1737–89), leader of the
famed Green Mountain Boys. This man's name became a
household word when he daringly stormed and captured
Fort Ticonderoga in 1775. Allen forced the commander to
surrender "in the name of the Great Jehovah and Continental Congress."

OLD CHARLESTON CHEESE-BRAN LOAF

2 small onions, minced	Pepper to taste
1 1/2 cups bran	2 cups cheese, grated
2 cups walnuts, chopped	Juice of 1 lemon
Salt to taste	3 eggs, well beaten
	1 cup bread crumbs

Fry the onions in butter until they are lightly browned.
Add 1/2 cup hot water to this. Then stir in the bran. Blend
in the walnuts next, then the salt, pepper, cheese, lemon
juice, and frothy beaten eggs. Beat together hard. Put the
mixture into a buttered baking dish. Sprinkle with the bread
crumbs. Bake in a hot oven (400 degrees) until browned.

Serve in the baking dish as soon as it is ready. Accompany with white cream gravy or some other good gravy.[4]

GREAT-GRANDMOTHER MITCHELL'S STUFFED ONIONS

6 large onions	Pinch of pepper
1 egg, hardboiled	Pinch of mace
1 cup bread crumbs, fine	3 tablespoons cream
1/2 teaspoon salt	1 egg, well beaten

Wash and skin the onions. Lay them in cold water for 1 hour. Then parboil them (partially cook) in boiling water for 1/2 hour. Drain, and while hot, extract the hearts. Take care not to break the outer layers. Chop the insides thus obtained very fine with the hardboiled egg. Add the rest of the ingredients and beat to a smooth paste. Stuff the onions with this mixture. Put them in a pan with a very little hot water. Place in the oven and simmer for 1 hour. Baste often with melted butter. When done, take the onions carefully up, and arrange the ends uppermost in a vegetable dish. Then take the juices in the pan and add:

4 tablespoons cream	Juice of 1/2 lemon
or	1 tablespoon flour, wet
4 tablespoons milk	in cold milk

Blend these well and then bring the mixture to a quick boil. Pour it over the stuffed onions. Serve while hot.

---

4. Recipes in Chapter 4.

EARLY VIRGINIA
NUTTY BAKED VEGETABLE CASSEROLE

1 cup onion, chopped

1 cup celery, chopped

1 cup parsley, chopped

2 tablespoons butter

Salt to taste

Pepper to taste

1 cup tomatoes, stewed

Juice of 1/2 lemon

1 1/2 cups bread crumbs

1 cup walnuts, chopped

2 eggs, well beaten

1 cup cheese, grated

Fry the onions, celery, and parsley in the butter until slightly browned. Then add the salt, pepper, tomatoes, lemon juice, bread crumbs, and walnuts. Stir well and then add the frothy beaten eggs. Pour into a well-buttered baking dish. Sprinkle with the grated cheese. Bake in a moderate oven (350 degrees) for 1/2 hour, or until lightly browned. Serve in the baking dish while hot.

GREAT-GRANDMOTHER SHAW'S
STUFFED CABBAGE

Take the outer leaves off of 1 very large head of cabbage. Then lay the cabbage head in a kettle of boiling water for 10 minutes. When ready place it in a pan of ice water and set aside for 2 hours before stuffing. When chilled through, wrap the cabbage head with a wide cloth band. This will hold the head together when the core is cut out. Then remove the core with a thin, sharp knife. Cut a little deeper than the length of the middle finger. Excavate the center of the cabbage, without widening the mouth of the aperture, until you have room for about 1 cup of the stuffing. Then proceed to prepare the stuffing by blending the following ingredients:

1/4 cup bread crumbs
1/4 cup cabbage, minced
1 tablespoon onion,
    minced
Pinch of salt

Pinch of pepper
3 tablespoons green
    pepper, minced
Pinch of thyme

Fill the cavity in the cabbage with this mixture. Tie a wide cloth strip over the hole in the top. Lay the cabbage in a large saucepan with 2 cups white cream gravy.[5] Stew it gently until very tender. Then take the cabbage out, unbind carefully, and lay it in a deep dish. Bring the gravy to a quick boil and immediately pour it over the cabbage in the dish. Serve while hot.

PLANTATION-STYLE
TOMATOES WITH SCRAMBLED EGGS

1 tablespoon butter
3 slices onion
6 tomatoes, sliced
6 eggs

Salt to taste
Pepper to taste
6 slices toast,
    buttered

Put the butter in a frying pan and melt it. Add the slices of onion and cook until browned. Then put in the tomato slices in and fry until well cooked. Drop the eggs in and scramble well. Salt and pepper to suit taste. Serve on the slices of buttered toast.

GENERAL ROCHAMBEAU'S
FAVORITE STEWED MUSHROOMS

1 cup mushrooms

3 tablespoons cream

5. Recipe in Chapter 4.

1/2 teaspoon salt	Flour to suit
1 tablespoon butter	1 egg

Put the mushrooms in a porcelain saucepan and cover them with cold water. Bring to a boil and then stir gently for 15 minutes while simmering. Add the salt. Chop the butter into bits and roll in flour. Add this to the mushrooms. Boil for 4 minutes. Now whip the egg and cream together. Put this in the mixture and stir for 2 minutes without letting it boil.

or

1 cup mushrooms	1/4 cup drawn butter gravy[6]
1 cup milk, warm	1 tablespoon flour, wet in
1/2 teaspoon salt	cold milk
1/2 teaspoon pepper	1 egg, well beaten

Put the mushrooms in a porcelain saucepan and cover them with cold water. Bring to a boil and then stew gently for 10 minutes. Then strain off the water and add the warm milk in its place. Stew this for 5 minutes. Add the salt, pepper and drawn butter gravy. Thicken it with the wet flour and the frothy beaten egg. Pour into a bowl and serve immediately. *Note*: This recipe dates far back in our history. General Jean Rochambeau (1725–1807) teamed with Washington and DeGrasse to defeat Cornwallis at the Siege of Yorktown on October 19, 1781. He came to America with 6,000 men to aid the patriot cause in 1770. General Rochambeau preferred the second method of preparation over the first.

CIVIL WAR PERIOD NUTTY-CHEESE LOAF

4 tablespoons butter	1 teaspoon salt
4 teaspoons onion, chopped	1 teaspoon pepper

---

6. Recipe in Chapter 4.

2 cups walnuts, chopped   1 1/2 cups milk, hot
1 cup bread crumbs   3 tablespoons lemon juice
1 cup rice, cooked   4 eggs, well beaten
2 cups cheese, grated

Put the butter into a frying pan and melt it. Then put
in the onions and fry them until nicely browned. Take a
large wooden mixing bowl and blend the walnuts, bread
crumbs, rice, cheese, salt, pepper, and milk. Stir in the lemon juice and the previously fried onions. Lastly fold in the
frothy beaten eggs. Put the mixture into a well-buttered baking dish. Bake in a slow oven (300 degrees) for about 1
hour. Serve in the baking dish with any good gravy.[7]

GREAT-GREAT-GRANDMOTHER DANIELS'S
STUFFED POTATOES

6 large potatoes   1 teaspoon salt
3 teaspoons butter   1/2 teaspoon pepper
3 teaspoons cream   Milk to suit
3 teaspoons cheese,   6 eggs, well beaten
   grated

Take the potatoes and bake them in a hot oven (400
degrees) for 1 hour, or until soft. Then cut a round piece
off the top of each. Scrape out the inside carefully. Do not
break the skins. Set aside the empty cases with the pieces
cut from the tops. Mash the potatoes in a wooden mixing
bowl. When smooth work in the butter and cream. Season
with cheese, salt and pepper. Blend in enough milk to make
a soft creamy mixture. Put this in a saucepan and heat.
Stir to prevent burning. When scalding hot, blend in the
frothy beaten eggs. Bring to a quick boil. Fill the potato

---

7. Recipes in Chapter 4.

skins with the hot mixture. Replace the caps. Return them
to the oven (350 degrees) and bake for 3 minutes. When
they are done arrange on a napkin in a deep dish with the
caps uppermost. Cover with a fold of the napkin, and serve
while hot. *Note*: My Great-great-grandmother sometimes
would omit the eggs and put in a double quantity of cheese
instead. They are very good either way. Try both for an old-
time treat.

OLD BOSTONIAN MUSHROOM PORK CHOPS

1 pound mushrooms, chopped	1 cup bread crumbs, fresh
1 small onion, chopped	Salt to taste
1 small clove garlic, chopped	Pepper to taste
1/2 cup celery, chopped	2 tablespoons olive oil
1/2 cup carrots, chopped	2 eggs, well beaten
1/2 green pepper, chopped	1 egg yolk, well beaten

Blend all of the above ingredients in the sequence given.
Beat together thoroughly. Then shape into 1/2 inch thick patties. Form into the shape of pork chops. Lay them in a
well-buttered baking dish or pan. Baste with melted butter and bake in a moderate oven (350 degrees) for 30 minutes, or until nicely browned. Serve while hot.

EARLY MARYLAND MACARONI A LA CREME

4 cups macaroni	1 tablespoon butter
2 cups milk	1 egg, well beaten
Pinch of salt	1 cup cheese, grated
1 teaspoon flour	

Put the macaroni into a saucepan and cover with slightly salted boiling water. Stew gently for 10 minutes. Drain off the water. Put in 1 cup of the milk and the salt. Stew until the macaroni is tender. Put it in a deep dish, cover, and set aside. Now heat the other cup of milk in the saucepan. Bring it to a boil and thicken with the flour. Stir in the butter and lastly the frothy beaten egg. When this mixture thickens, pour it over the macaroni in the covered dish. Sprinkle the grated cheese thickly over it, or send around a saucer of grated cheese with it. *Note*: This is a simple and delicious main dish. Any leftover can be sprinkled with sugar and nutmeg or a nice sweet sauce.[8] Serve in this way as a tasty dessert dish.

EARLY TENNESSEE BAKED OMELET

1 tablespoon flour	Salt to taste
1 cup milk, cold	pepper to taste
1 cup milk, boiling	4 eggs, well beaten
1 tablespoon butter	

Smoothly blend the flour with the cold milk. Pour this into a saucepan containing the boiling milk. Stir over the fire until it thickens. Then add the butter, salt, and pepper. Stir well and then blend this mixture into the frothy beaten eggs. Whip everything together hard. Pour into a buttered pudding dish. Bake in a moderate oven (350 degrees) for 20 minutes. *Note*: In making an old-fashioned baked omelet puff, beat the egg yolks and egg whites separately. Add the fluffy whites last, and stir them in lightly.

MRS. CALHOUN'S STUFFED BAKED TOMATOES

6 large tomatoes	1/2 teaspoon pepper
1 cup bread crumbs	1 teaspoon sugar

8. Recipes in Chapter 4.

1/4 cup green corn	1 tablespoon butter
1 teaspoon salt	1 egg, well beaten

Cut a thin slice from the blossom end of each tomato and set it aside. Scoop out the insides of each tomato. Put the scrapings in a wooden mixing bowl and blend with the rest of the ingredients. Beat together hard and then stuff the hollowed tomatoes. Fit the tops neatly back on each tomato. Place them in a deep buttered baking dish. Bake in a moderate oven (350 degrees) for 3/4 hour, or until slightly browned. Serve while hot. *Note*: This was a delightful dish that often graced the table in the home of John Calhoun, vice-president under John Quincy Adams from 1825 to 1829, and vice-president under Andrew Jackson from 1829 to 1837. Mrs. Calhoun sometimes made it without the egg. It is good either way.

PRIZE OLD-FASHIONED
PEANUT BUTTER-RICE STEAKS

1 cup rice, boiled	1 teaspoon onion, grated
1 cup bread crumbs	1/4 cup catsup[9]
1/2 cup peanut butter	Pinch of dry mustard
1 teaspoon celery salt	2 eggs, well beaten

Combine all of the above ingredients in a large wooden mixing bowl. Blend well and then form into 1/2-inch-thick cakes. Place each steak in a buttered baking dish. Bake in a moderate oven (350 degrees) for about 1/2 hour, or until nicely browned. Baste at least once while they are baking. Serve while hot. *Note*: Fresh ground roasted peanuts may be substituted for the peanut butter if desired. This makes the finished steak a little more crunchy.

---

9. Recipes in *Natural Cooking the Old Fashioned Way*, by the author.

GRANDMOTHER PELTON'S CHEESE SOUFFLE

2 tablespoons butter	3 egg yolks, well beaten
1 1/2 tablespoons flour	1 cup cheese, grated
1/2 cup milk	3 egg whites, stiffly
Pinch of salt	beaten
Pinch of red pepper	

Put the butter into a saucepan and heat. Stir in the flour until it is a smooth cream. Then add the milk, salt, and pepper. Simmer for 2 minutes. Whip in the frothy beaten egg yolks and the grated cheese. Set aside to cool. When cold fold in the stiffly beaten egg whites. Turn into a buttered baking dish. Put in a moderate oven (350 degrees) and bake for 25 to 30 minutes. *Note*: This souffle will rise quite high. It should be served without delay or it will quickly fall on cooling.

OLD NEW ORLEANS BAKED MACARONI

2 cups macaroni	4 eggs, hardboiled and
2 cups cheese, grated	sliced
1 cup ripe olives,	1/4 cup butter
halved	1/4 cup cream
Salt to suit	

Put the macaroni into a saucepan of slightly salted boiling water. Simmer it gently for 20 minutes. It should be soft, but not broken or split. Drain well and put a layer of it in the bottom of a buttered baking dish. Sprinkle some of the cheese over this. Then add some of the olives, a little salt, and some eggs. Scatter bits of butter over all of this. Lay down more macaroni. Then cheese, olives, salt, eggs, and butter. Continue this procedure until the dish is filled. The last layer should be macaroni, buttered well. Pour the cream over the top and cover the dish. Bake in a moderate oven (350 degrees) for 1/2 hour. Then remove the cover and let it brown nicely. Serve while hot.

GRANDMOTHER COLLISTER'S GREEN PEPPER CASSEROLE

2 green peppers, chopped fine	Pinch of pepper
1 stalk celery, chopped fine	3 1/2 cups rice, cooked
	3 tablespoons catsup[10]
1 small onion, minced	1 cup tomatoes, stewed
	1 tablespoon lemon juice
1 teaspoon salt	Pinch of dry mustard
	Bread crumbs to suit

Melt enough butter to cover the bottom of a large frying pan. Put in the green peppers, celery and onion. Fry them until the onion browns. Stir in the salt, pepper and cooked rice. Blend well and add the catsup, tomatoes, lemon juice and dry mustard. Stir thoroughly and pour into a buttered baking dish. Sprinkle bread crumbs over the top. Bake in a moderate oven (350 degrees) for about 30 minutes, or until firm and browned. Serve in the baking dish while hot.

UNRIVALED OLD-TIME BEAN LOAF

3 cups kidney beans, cooked	1/2 teaspoon paprika
	1 tablespoon flour
2 cups cheese, grated	2 tablespoons butter, melted
1 onion, chopped	

10. Recipes in *Natural Cooking the Old Fashioned Way*, by the author.

| 1/2 teaspoon salt | 3 eggs, well beaten |
| 1/2 teaspoon pepper | 2 cups bread crumbs |

Drain the beans well and mash them through a colander. Add the grated cheese and stir until it melts. Quickly fry the onion in a little hot butter until it browns. Combine these with the bean-cheese paste mixture. Then stir in the seasonings, flour, butter, and frothy beaten eggs. Add 1 cup of the bread crumbs. Mix well and form into a loaf. Baste it with water and melted butter. Roll the loaf in bread crumbs. Pack it firmly into a buttered loaf pan or baking dish and sprinkle with the remaining bread crumbs. Bake in a moderate oven (350 degrees) for about 1/2 hour. Serve in the baking dish while hot. Accompany with any good gravy.[11]

GENERAL BRAGG'S
FAVORITE ASPARAGUS IN AMBUSH

50 asparagus tips, fresh	2 cups milk
12 biscuits,[12] stale	4 eggs, well beaten
or	2 tablespoons butter
12 rolls,[13] stale	1/2 teaspoon salt
	1 2 teaspoon pepper

Put the asparagus tips in a kettle and cover them with water. Bring this to a boil and then simmer until they are tender. Drain and set aside when done. Now take the stale biscuits or rolls and cut a slice from the top of each one. Scrape out some of the insides. Set them in a baking pan and lay the tops alongside. Put into a moderate oven (350 degrees) to crisp nicely.

---

11. Recipes in Chapter 4.
12. Recipes in *Natural Baking the Old Fashioned Way,* by the author.
13. Ibid.

Meanwhile put the milk into a saucepan and bring it to a boil. Then whip in the frothy beaten eggs. Simmer and stir until it thickens. Then stir in the butter, salt, and pepper. Lastly mince the cooked asparagus tips and stir them into this mixture. Immediately remove from the stove.

Take the crisped biscuits or rolls from the oven. Fill them with some of this custardlike mixture. Put the tops carefully back on each. Set in the oven again for 3 minutes. Then take out and arrange them on a dish or platter. Serve while hot. *Note*: This is an excellent main course. Cheese can be added if desired, just before adding the asparagus to the custard blend above. "Asparagus in Ambush" was made by Mrs. Bragg for her son General Braxton Bragg (1817–76). He was the Confederate general defeated at Chattanooga, Tennessee, by General Grant on November 23, 1863. Bragg was then soundly whipped by General Hooker at Lookout Mountain the very next day, and at Missionary Ridge by General Sherman on Thanksgiving Day. He was later appointed as military advisor to Jefferson Davis in February of 1864.

3

Exciting Old-time Natural Side Dishes

GREAT-GREAT-GRANDMOTHER HORTON'S LADIES' CABBAGE

1 head cabbage, large
    and firm
2 eggs, well beaten
1 tablespoon butter,
    melted

1 tablespoon pepper
1 tablespoon salt
3 tablespoons cream
    or
3 tablespoons milk

Put the head of cabbage into a kettle and cover it with boiling water. Simmer it for 15 minutes. Then pour off the water and add some fresh boiling water from the tea kettle. Cook until the cabbage is tender. Then drain it and set the cabbage head aside until cool. When completely cold chop it up fine. Put it into a wooden mixing bowl. Add the frothy beaten eggs, melted butter, seasoning, and cream or milk. Whip all these ingredients together thoroughly. Pour into a well-buttered baking dish. Bake in a moderate oven (350 degrees) until browned. Serve while very hot. *Note*: I can conscientiously recommend this dish even to those who are not overly fond of any of the ordinary preparations of cabbage. It is easily digestible and palatable, nearly resembling cauliflower in taste. Try it yourself and see.

STEWED CUCUMBERS—
A FAVORITE OF BENEDICT ARNOLD

3 large cucumbers	1/2 cup cream
Salt to taste	or
Pepper to taste	1/2 cup milk
2 tablespoons butter	2 tablespoons flour
	1 tablespoon lemon juice

Pare the cucumbers and lay them in a bowl of ice water for 1 hour. Then slice them in 1/4-inch-thick-pieces. Pick out all the seeds with a pointed knife. Put the slices into a saucepan with enough boiling water to cover them. Stew for 15 minutes. Then drain off the water. Add enough fresh boiling water to keep them from burning. Season with salt and pepper to taste. Carefully stir in the butter until it all melts. Simmer gently for another 10 minutes. Add the cream or milk. Thicken with the flour. Bring to a quick boil and immediately pour the mixture into a deep serving dish. Stir in the lemon juice last and serve while hot. *Note*: This was a popular old-fashioned English dish, although it may seem somewhat strange to American ideas. It was a favorite of Benedict Arnold (1741–1801). This man fought with the American forces and defeated St. Leger at Fort Stanwix on August 22, 1777. But three years later he changed his loyalties and tried to surrender West Point to the British. This infamous American later became a British colonel. His treasonous act has never been forgiven—not even two centuries later.

OLD VIRGINIA BUTTERED PARSNIPS

6 large parsnips
3 tablespoons butter,
    melted
Salt to taste

Pepper to taste
Pinch of parsley
3 tablespoons cream

Put the parsnips into a kettle and just cover with water. Bring to a boil and then let it simmer until they are tender. Then drain and scrape off the skin. Slice the parsnips lengthwise in 1/4-inch-thick strips. Put the slices into a saucepan with the melted butter and seasonings. Shake or stir over the fire until the mixture boils. Immediately remove the parsnips and lay them on a warm serving dish. Stir the cream into the gravy in the saucepan. Bring it to a quick boil and pour over the parsnips in the dish. Garnish with more parsley and serve while hot.

EARLY ALABAMA SPINACH A LA CREME

8 cups spinach, boiled
    and chopped fine
Salt to taste
Pepper to taste

3 tablespoons butter,
    melted
3 tablespoons cream
1 teaspoon sugar
4 eggs, hard-boiled

Heat the spinach in a saucepan and season it with the salt and pepper. Beat in the melted butter. Stir constantly until it becomes smoking hot. Then stir in the cream and sugar. Bring to a quick boil. Press firmly into a hot bowl or other mold. Then turn this onto a hot dish and garnish with sliced hard-boiled eggs.

GREAT-GRANDMOTHER MITCHELL'S
BROCCOLI AND EGGS

3 heads broccoli   2 cups drawn butter gravy[1]
4 eggs, well beaten   4 slices toast, buttered

Put the broccoli into a saucepan with enough water to cover it. Simmer until tender. Heat the drawn butter gravy in another saucepan, and when smoking hot, whip the frothy beaten eggs into it. Lay the buttered toast on the bottom of a hot serving dish. Put the largest whole head of broccoli on this as a center piece. Cut the rest of the broccoli into small clusters. Lay these pieces around the center piece, stems facing downward. Pour the hot egg sauce over the broccoli and serve immediately.

CIVIL WAR ERA STEWED CAULIFLOWER

2 heads cauliflower   2 tablespoons butter,
1/2 cup milk   melted
1 tablespoon rice flour   Pinch of salt
                           Pinch of pepper

Cut the cauliflower in small bunches or clusters and lay them in a pan of cold, salted water. Leave for 1/2 hour. Then drain and just cover with fresh water. Bring to a boil and let it simmer for 15 minutes. Drain off all but 1/2 cup of the hot water. Thicken the milk with the rice flour and pour this over the cauliflower. Stir in the melted butter and the seasonings. Shake the saucepan over the fire gently until the mixture boils. Then take out the cauliflower with a perforated skimmer. Lay the clusters on a hot serving dish. Pour the sauce over them. Serve while hot. *Note*: In the

1. Recipe in Chapter 4.

early days, the smaller and "indifferent" heads of cauliflower were used in this recipe so as not to waste them.

COLONIAL-STYLE GREEN PEAS

Shell your fresh green peas. Put them into a kettle of cold water until you are ready to cook. When ready, drain the peas and put them into a kettle of salted boiling water. Let them simmer for 20 to 30 minutes. If the peas are young and very fresh, the shorter time will suffice. If just gathered from your own vines and tender, season only with salt. Market peas are greatly improved by the addition of a teaspoon of sugar. It improves their taste and color. Drain the peas well and dish up while hot. Stir in a large lump of butter and a little pepper. Cover the dish to keep the peas hot. *Note*: This was a popular colonial dish. In those days the English always put in a sprig of mint. This was removed when the peas were dished and served.

GENERAL GATES'S
FAVORITE POTATO CROQUETTES

4 cups potatoes, boiled and mashed	Nutmeg to taste
	4 tablespoons butter, melted
Salt to taste	6 eggs, well beaten
Pepper to taste	1 tablespoon parsley

Put the cold mashed potatoes into a wooden mixing bowl. Stir in the seasonings. Then add the butter and beat to a very smooth and creamy mixture. Blend in the frothy beaten eggs and the parsley. Form the mixture into egg-sized oval balls with floured hands. Dip each ball in beaten egg and then roll it in bread crumbs. Deep fry until lightly browned. Pile the croquettes in a pyramid on a flat dish. Serve while hot. *Note*: General Horatio Gates (1728-1806) had a special love for potato croquettes made in this way. He served under General Braddock and was severely wounded at Fort Duquesne in 1755. He retired to Virginia from 1763 to 1775. As an American general during the Revolutionary War he defeated British troops under General Burgoyne at Saratoga on October 17, 1777.

COUNTRY MASHED TURNIPS IN EARLY MISSISSIPPI

6 large turnips	Pepper to taste
3 tablespoons butter, melted	3 tablespoons cream or
Salt to taste	3 tablespoons milk

Peel the raw turnips and lay them in a pan of cold, salted water for 15 minutes. Then put them into a kettle with just enough water to cover. Bring this to a boil and then let it simmer until the turnips are tender. The time this takes will depend upon their age. When tender drain the turnips and mash them through a colander with a wooden spoon. Put the mashed turnips into a saucepan. Stir in the melted butter, seasonings, and the cream or milk. Bring to a quick boil and serve immediately.

GREAT-GREAT-GRANDMOTHER HORTON'S HOMEMADE SAUERKRAUT

Shred or chop up the cabbage fine. Line a barrel, keg, or large stone jar with cabbage leaves on the bottom and sides. Put in a 3 inch layer of the cut cabbage. Press down well and sprinkle with 4 tablespoons salt. Pack 5 layers in this way. Then press hard with a board cut to fit loosely on the inside of the barrel or jar. Put heavy weights on this, or pound it down with a wooden beetle until the cabbage is a compact mass. Then remove the board and put in 5 more layers of salt and shredded cabbage. Repeat the pounding. Continue this sequence until the vessel is full. Then cover with cabbage leaves. Put the round board on top of these with a heavy weight to keep it tightly down. Set the vessel aside to ferment. In 3 weeks remove the scum. Cover the cabbage with water if needed. Keep in a cool, dry place (the cellar if you have one). The sauerkraut can be eaten raw or boiled.

This is a simple method of preparing delicious old-fashioned homemade sauerkraut. Some old-timers added 2 whole peppercorns, whole cloves, mace, and chunks of garlic with each sprinkling of salt. *Note*: A fair warning! This is a malodorous compound to nostrils unaccustomed to it. Many years ago, a mild, motherly Teuton dame was telling my great-great-grandmother what to do with the cabbage mixture after it was all put together. She said: "Then put it away in the cellar to r. . . ." "Rot!" interpolated a disgusted bystander, anticipating her deliberate utterance. "No, my dear," drawled the placid Frau, "to *ripen*."

BOILED BEETS IN EARLY GEORGIA

Wash the beets and put them into a kettle of boiling water. Cook them until they are tender. This will take about 2 hours if the beets are full grown. When done, drain well, and rub off the skins. If the beets are large slice them. If very young and small beets are used simply split them. Put into a serving bowl and melt butter over them. Stir well and add salt and pepper to taste. Serve while hot.

or

Slice the cooked beets and lay them in the bowl. Then take the saucepan and blend:

3 tablespoons butter,	1/4 teaspoon pepper
melted	4 tablespoons cider vinegar[2]
1/2 teaspoon salt	

Bring this mixture to a boil and quickly pour it over the hot beets in the bowl. *Note*: Never cut beets before they are boiled. If cut while raw they will bleed themselves pale in the hot water. Instead of consigning cold "leftover" beets to the garbage, pour cold vinegar over them and use as pickles at another meal.

GREAT-GRANDMOTHER MITCHELL'S RICE CROQUETTES

1/2 cup rice	Pinch of salt
2 cups milk	3 eggs, well beaten
2 tablespoons sugar	1/2 lemon rind,
1 tablespoon butter,	grated
melted	

Put the rice into a saucepan with just enough *warm* water to cover it. Leave it to soak for 3 hours. Then drain and pour in the milk. Set the pan into a larger kettle of boiling water. Stew the rice until it is very tender. When tender add the sugar, butter, and salt. Simmer for 10 minutes. Take the saucepan from the fire and whip the frothy beaten eggs into the mixture. Return the pan to the stove and stir until it thickens well. *Do not allow it to boil.* Remove the saucepan again and stir in the grated lemon peel. Then turn the mixture out on a well-buttered dish to cool. When cold and stiff, flour your hands and roll into small oval or pear-shaped balls. Dip each ball into some beaten egg and then roll in fine cracker crumbs. Deep fry until

2. Recipe in *Natural Cooking the Old Fashioned Way*, by the author.

lightly browned. Serve while hot. *Note:* In early days, when the rice mixture was shaped like a pear, a clove was inserted into the small end for the stem.

ORIGINAL NEW ENGLAND BAKED ONIONS

The large Spanish or Bermuda onions were the only kinds used for baking in the old days. Wash the onions but *do not* remove the skins. Heat a kettle of slightly salted boiling water and then put in the onions. Let them cook for 20 minutes. Then empty out the water and replenish it with fresh, slightly salted boiling water. Cook for 20 minutes longer. Change the water again and cook for 20 more minutes. Take the onions out of the kettle and set them on a towel. Leave them until all the moisture has been absorbed or it evaporates. Then roll each onion in a piece of buttered tissue paper. Twist it at the top to keep it closed. Put them in a shallow buttered baking pan. Bake in a slow oven (300 degrees) for 1 hour.

Now take the onions from the oven, remove the tissue paper, and peel them. Lay them in a deep, buttered baking dish. Baste freely with melted butter and bake for 15 minutes, or until they are slightly browned. Put them in a serving bowl and sprinkle with salt and pepper. Pour the melted butter from the baking dish over them. Serve immediately.

GENERAL MARION'S
FAVORITE ROAST SWEET POTATOES

Select sweet potatoes of uniform size. Wash, wipe, and roast until you can tell, by gently pressing the largest part between the finger and thumb, that they are mellow throughout. Serve in their jackets. Sweet, as well as white, potatoes are very good for picnics, when roasted in hot ashes. This, it should be remembered, was the dinner General Marion set before the British officer as "quite a feast, I assure you, sir. We don't often fare so well as to have sweet potatoes and salt." *Note*: The "feast" was cleansed from ashes by the Negro orderly's shirt-sleeve, and served upon a natural trencher of pine bark.

EARLY SOUTHERN PLANTATION OKRA

Put the okra pods into a kettle of salted boiling water. Cook them until nice and tender. Drain thoroughly and put into a serving bowl. Quickly blend the following in a saucepan:

4 tablespoons butter, melted	Salt to taste
1 tablespoon vinegar[3]	Pepper to taste

Heat this to the boiling point. Immediately pour it over the hot okra in the bowl. Serve while hot. *Note*: About 2 pounds okra should be sufficient. More can be used if desired.

ARTICHOKES IN OLD NEW ENGLAND HOMES

Strip off the outer leaves. Cut the stalks close to the bottom. Wash well and lay them in cold water for 2 hours. Then immerse in boiling water the stalk ends uppermost. Lay an inverted plate on them to keep down under the water. Simmer for 1 1/2 hours, or until very tender. Arrange

---

3. Recipes in *Natural Cooking the Old Fashioned Way*, by the author.

in circles on a dish, the tops up. Pour drawn butter gravy[4] over them. Serve while hot.

GREAT-GREAT-GRANDMOTHER NORTHRUP'S FRIED CUCUMBERS

Pare the desired number of cucumbers and lay them in ice water for 1/2 hour. Then cut lengthwise into slices nearly 1/2 inch thick. Lay the slices back in the ice water for 10 more minutes. Then wipe each piece dry with a soft cloth. Sprinkle with salt and pepper. Dredge (sprinkle) heavily with flour. Fry in hot butter until each piece is a delicate brown on both sides. *Note*: My great-great-grandmother declared that cucumbers are "never fit to eat unless fried, and they are assuredly far more wholesome than when served raw."

SCALLOPED CAULIFLOWER ON THE OLD LOUISIANA BAYOU

2 heads cauliflower	Pepper to taste
1 cup bread crumbs	3 tablespoons cream
2 tablespoons butter,	or
melted	3 tablespoons milk
Salt to taste	1 egg, well beaten

Put the cauliflower into a large kettle and cover with water. Boil until tender. Then drain well, and clip into neat clusters. Pack, with the stems downward, in a well-buttered baking dish. Then put the bread crumbs in a wooden mixing bowl. Add the melted butter, seasoning, and cream or milk. Beat hard. When it is a smooth paste add the frothy

---

4. Recipe in Chapter 4.

beaten egg. Stir well and spread this mixture over the cauliflower in the dish. Cover the dish closely. Put in the oven and bake for 6 minutes at 400 degrees. Then remove the cover and brown for 5 more minutes. Serve while very hot in the baking dish.

ORIGINAL EARLY AMERICAN CHEESE STICKS

2 cups flour	1 cup cheese, grated
1/4 cup butter	Pinch of red pepper

Blend all of the above ingredients together in a wooden mixing bowl. Add enough water to make a soft, pliable dough. Roll the dough out in a 1/8-inch- to 1/4 inch-thick sheet (thicker if desired). Cut it in narrow 6-inch-long strips. Lay the strips on a buttered and floured shallow baking pan. Bake in a moderate oven (350 degrees) until they turn a light brown. *Note*: These old-fashioned cheese sticks are delicious when served either hot or cold. They were popular on the Western frontier as well as in the finer homes of the Old South.

BAKED PUMPKIN
FAVORITE OF GENERAL SHERMAN

Choose the richest pumpkin you can find and cut it in quarters or eighths. Take out all the seeds. Pare and slice lengthwise 1/2 inch thick. Arrange in layers—not more than 2 or 3 slices deep—in a shallow but broad baking dish. Put a *very* little water in the bottom. Bake very slowly (250 to 275 degrees) until not only done, but dry. It requires a long time for the heat must be gentle. Butter each strip on both sides when you dish and serve them. In the old days this was eaten hot with bread and butter for teas, luncheons, and as a side dish for dinner. It is an extremely palatable dish. Try it if you are fond of the flavor of pumpkin. *Note*: General William Tecumseh Sherman (1820–91) had this pumpkin dish prepared especially for him by his orderlies. He gained fame for his now-famous march to the sea during the Civil War era. Sherman defeated Hood during the Siege of Atlanta from July 22 to September 2, 1864. He then took Savannah in December. And Charleston was occupied by his Union troops on February 18, 1865, when he soundly thrashed General Beauregard.

FRIED PARSNIPS IN THE COLONIES

Put some fresh parsnips into a kettle of water and boil them until tender. Then drain, wipe dry, and scrape off the skin. Cut into 1/4-inch-thick lengthwise slices. Wet the slices and dredge (sprinkle) with flour. Fry in hot butter. Turn when one side has browned and brown the other. Then put the slices on a napkin and drain off the butter. Sprinkle with pepper and serve while hot.

OLD SOUTHERN STEWED BEETS

12 young beets	Pinch of pepper
1 scallion, minced	2 tablespoons butter,
1/2 teaspoon parsley	melted
Pinch of salt	2 tablespoons vinegar[5]

Put the young, sweet beets into a kettle of boiling water. Simmer slowly until nearly done. Then drain well. Skin and slice the beets. Put the slices in a saucepan with the rest

---

5. Recipes in *Natural Cooking the Old Fashioned Way*, by the author.

of the ingredients. Let it all simmer for 20 minutes. Shake the saucepan now and then to prevent burning. Serve while hot with the saucepan gravy poured over them.

GREAT-GREAT-GRANDMOTHER DANIELS'S HOMINY CROQUETTES

4 cups hominy, boiled and cold	4 cups milk
	4 teaspoons sugar
4 tablespoons butter melted	4 eggs, well beaten

Put the cold hominy into a large wooden mixing bowl and stir in the melted butter. Beat hard. Moisten, by degrees, with the milk. Beat the mixture to a soft, light paste. Then add the sugar. Lastly whip in the frothy beaten eggs. Form the mixture into egg-sized oval balls with floured hands. Dip each hominy ball in beaten egg and then roll it in cracker crumbs. Deep fry until lightly browned. Serve while hot.

FRIED EGG PLANT ON THE PLANTATION

Slice the eggplant at least 1/2 inch thick. Pare each piece carefully. Lay them in cold salted water. Put a plate on the slices to keep them under the brine. Set aside for at least 1 hour or more. Then wipe each slice. Dip in beaten egg. Then roll the slices in cracker crumbs. Deep fry until well done and nicely browned. Let them drain for a moment. Serve while hot.

ORIGINAL OLDEN-DAY POTATO PUFF

2 cups potatoes,	3/4 cup cream

cold and mashed
2 tablespoons butter, melted
2 eggs, well beaten

or
3/4 cup milk
Salt to taste
Pepper to taste

Take the cold mashed potatoes and put into a wooden mixing bowl. Stir in the melted butter. Beat this to a white cream before adding anything else. Then whip in the frothy beaten eggs and the cream or milk. Salt and pepper to suit taste. Beat the entire mixture long and hard. Then pour it into a deep, buttered baking dish. Bake in a quick oven (400 degrees) until it is nicely browned. *Note*: If properly mixed and baked, this will come out of the oven light, puffy, and delectable.

CLINTON'S FAVORITE BAKED HOMINY DISH

4 cups hominy, boiled
12 egg yolks, well beaten
3 tablespoons butter, melted
1 1/2 tablespoons sugar

1/2 teaspoon salt
2 quarts milk
12 egg whites, stiffly beaten

Put the cold, boiled hominy into a large wooden mixing bowl. Work the frothy beaten egg yolks into it, alternately with the butter. When thoroughly blended put in the sugar and salt. Continue beating while you gradually soften the batter with the milk. Be careful to leave no lumps in the hominy. Lastly and lightly stir in the fluffy egg whites. Put this mixture into a buttered baking dish. Bake in a moderate oven (350 degrees) until light, firm, and delicately browned. *Note*: This can be eaten as a dessert, but it is a delightful vegetable dish. Mrs. Clinton considered it to be "the best substitute that can be devised for green corn pudding." She was the mother of George Clinton, a man often forgotten in history. Few can remember him. This man was vice-president under Thomas Jefferson in 1805 and James Madison in 1809.

CHARLESTON BLACKS'
OLD-TIME CREAMED SWEET POTATOES

6 sweet potatoes, medium sized	Juice of 1 orange
1 teaspoon salt	Juice of 1/2 lemon
1/2 cup brown sugar	1 tablespoon orange rind, grated
1/2 teaspoon cinnamon	1/2 lemon rind, grated
Pinch of nutmeg	2 eggs, well beaten
1/4 cup butter, melted	1 cup cream, whipped

Put the sweet potatoes into a kettle with just enough water to cover them. Boil until they are tender. When done, drain well, and scrape off the skins. Put the sweet potatoes in a large wooden mixing bowl and mash them. Beat hard until they are smooth and creamy. Then whip in the salt, sugar, and spices. Next beat in the melted butter, juices, and rinds. Lastly whip in the frothy beaten eggs. Put this mixture into a buttered baking dish. Bake in a moderate oven (350 degrees) for about 30 minutes, or until the top begins to slightly brown. Then take from the oven and cover with the thick whipped cream. Serve immediately. *Note*: This potato mixture should be just thick enough to mold but not overly stiff. If too stiff, add a little milk to thin it down.

EARLY NEW ENGLAND BOILED SEA KALE

Pick the sea kale over carefully. Tie up in bunches and lay them in cold water for 1 hour. Then put into salted boiling water. Cook for 3 minutes or until tender. Lay some slices of buttered toast in the bottom of a dish. Clip the threads binding the stems of the sea kale. Pile on top of the toast. Butter it abundantly. Or, you can send it around with a boat[6] of drawn butter gravy.[7]

GREAT-GRANDMOTHER SHAW'S MASHED PARSNIPS

6 large parsnips	2 tablespoons butter
4 tablespoons cream	Salt to taste
or	Pepper to taste
4 tablespoons milk	

Put the parsnips into a kettle of water and boil until they are tender. Then drain well, and scrape off the skin. Mash the parsnips with the back of a large wooden spoon. Pick out all of the stringy fibers. Blend in the cream or milk, butter, and seasonings. Put this mixture into a saucepan and bring it to a boil. Beat hard. Heap into a mound in a bowl. Serve while hot.

OLD ATLANTA PLANTATION-STYLE SUCCOTASH

3 cups green corn	1 teaspoon flour
2 cups lima beans	Salt to taste
1 1/4 cups milk	Pepper to taste
2 tablespoons butter	

Put the corn and lima beans into a saucepan with just enough water to cover them. Stew gently for 1/2 hour. Stir occasionally. Then pour off all the water. Add the milk

---

6. Table dish for gravy.
7. Recipe in Chapter 4.

to the corn-bean mixture in the saucepan. Simmer for 1 hour. Watch carefully and stir occasionally to prevent burning. Then stir in the butter. Wet the flour in a little cold milk and stir it in. Season to taste with salt and pepper. Bring to a quick boil and pour into a deep vegetable dish. Serve while hot. *Note*: String beans or butter beans can be substituted for the lima beans. If string beans are used, string them and cut into 1/2-inch lengths before cooking.

CUSTER'S FAVORITE FRIED TOMATOES

6 large green tomatoes	1 cup cream
Salt to taste	or
Pepper to taste	1 cup milk
Flour to taste	1 tablespoon butter, melted

Peel and slice the green tomatoes. Salt and pepper each slice liberally. Then dip in flour until each slice is thickly covered. Fy in hot butter until nicely browned. Drain the fried slices on brown paper. When all the slices are fried and draining, put the cream or milk into the frying pan. Add 1 tablespoon flour to thicken it. Stir in the butter. Salt and pepper to suit taste. Stir well. Put the tomatoes into a bowl. Pour this mixture over them. Serve immediately. *Note*: Green tomatoes fried in this way are delicious when served without the pan gravy as above. Ripe tomatoes can also be fried for a totally different taste variation. General George Armstrong Custer (1839–76) enjoyed this particular dish often in his lifetime. His mother usually made it with the green tomatoes, since this was George's favorite. Custer first gained fame as an Indian fighter in General W. S. Hancock's campaign against the Cheyennes from 1867 to 1868. His forces were later wiped out by Sitting Bull's warriors at Little Big Horn.

4

Tasty Gravy and Sauces with Natural Foods

EARLY PLANTATION EGG SAUCE GRAVY

3 eggs, hard-boiled   Salt to taste
1 cup drawn butter gravy,[1]   Pinch of parsley
    hot   1 scallion, minced

Chop the yolks and whites of the eggs until they are very
fine. Put into a wooden mixing bowl and then beat in the
hot drawn butter gravy. Salt to suit taste and stir in the
parsley. Lastly add the minced scallion. *Note*: Many old-
timers also added chopped pickle, capers, or nasturtium
seeds for a delightful variation of this sauce. Others liked
to use only the chopped egg yolks rather than both the
whites and yolks.

---

1. Recipe included herein.

GREAT-GRANDMOTHER MITCHELL'S
ASPARAGUS GRAVY

12 asparagus tips	Pinch of salt
1 1/2 cups drawn butter	Pinch of white pepper
gravy,[2] hot	Juice of 1/2 lemon
2 eggs	

Boil the asparagus tips in very little salted water until they are tender. Drain well and then chop them up fine. Beat the eggs into the hot drawn butter gravy. Then stir the asparagus tips into this. Blend in the salt and pepper. Lastly add the lemon juice. *Note*: The drawn butter gravy should be very hot. Do not cook this mixture after putting in the asparagus tips.

COLONIAL ERA SWEETENED CREAM

2 cups cream	1 teaspoon nutmeg
4 tablespoons powdered	1 teaspoon vanilla
sugar	

Blend all of the above ingredients together in a wooden mixing bowl. Stir until the sugar is completely dissolved. Set on ice to chill. Serve when cold with all types puddings, cakes, and pies.

GENERAL BEAUREGARD'S
FAVORITE FRUIT PUDDING SAUCE

1/2 cup butter	1 cup water, boiling
2 1/2 cups sugar	Juice of 1 lemon

---

2. Recipe included herein.

3/4 tablespoons corn   1/2 lemon rind, grated
    starch   1/4 cup wine

Beat the butter and sugar together in a wooden mixing bowl until light and creamy. Wet the cornstarch in a little cold milk. Stir it into the boiling water until thick. Then pour this mixture into the butter-sugar cream mixture in the bowl. Add the lemon juice and grated rind. Beat hard for 5 full minutes before returning it to the saucepan. Heat it to almost boiling. Stir in the wine and serve while hot. *Note*: General Pierre Beauregard (1818–93) had a special liking for this type of pudding sauce. This man was in charge of the Confederate troops that started the Civil War by firing on Fort Sumter, April 12, 1861. He fought and lost in the defense of Charleston against Sherman's forces in 1863. Beauregard later managed the infamous Louisiana Lottery.

BREAD GRAVY
DURING THE REVOLUTIONARY WAR PERIOD

1 onion, sliced   Salt to taste
2 cups milk   Pinch of mace
1 cup bread crumbs,   Pepper to taste
    very fine   3 tablespoon butter

Put the onion and milk into a saucepan and simmer together until tender. Strain the hot milk over the bread crumbs. Cover and let soak for 1/2 hour. Then beat until smooth and creamy. Add the seasoning and butter. Stir well and put back into another saucepan. Bring to a quick boil and immediately pour into a tureen.[3] Serve while steaming hot.
Note: If this gravy is too thick, add a little boiling water and more butter to the mixture.

-----

3. Table dish for gravy.

ORIGINAL EARLY AMERICAN
BUTTERSCOTCH SAUCE

2 cups sugar   1 cup cream, hot
1 cup butter

Cream the sugar and butter together in a saucepan. Heat and let it gently simmer until light brown in color. Then blend in the hot cream and stir until smooth. Pour into a small serving bowl. Serve while warm with fresh coconut pudding[4] or any other pudding or dessert[5] of your choice.

GREAT-GREAT-GRANDMOTHER NORTHRUP'S
OLD-TIME JELLY SAUCE

2 tablespoons butter,   1/2 lemon rind, grated
   melted   1/2 teaspoon nutmeg
1/2 cup currant jelly[6]   1/2 cup wine
Juice of 1 lemon   1 tablespoon powdered sugar

Put the butter into a saucepan and heat until it is luke-warm. Beat the jelly until it is a smooth paste and add to the warm melted butter. Then stir in the lemon juice, rind, and nutmeg. Warm to almost a boil. Set the saucepan in a larger vessel of hot water. Keep covered to prevent the escape of the wine flavor. Stir occasionally. Stir well just before pouring into a serving bowl. Serve immediately while hot. *Note*: This is a very fine sauce for all kinds of old-fashioned puddings.

---

4. Recipe in Chapter 14.
5. Ibid.
6. Recipe in *Natural Cooking the Old Fashioned Way*, by the author.

EARLY SOUTHERN WHITE CREAM GRAVY

1 tablespoon butter, well rounded	1/4 teaspoon salt
2 tablespoons flour	1 cup milk

Put the butter into a saucepan and melt it. Remove from the fire and thoroughly blend in the flour and salt. Lastly stir in the milk. Return the saucepan to the stove and stir constantly as it simmers. Continue cooking until the gravy bubbles and thickens. When done pour into a bowl and garnish with paprika and parsley. Serve hot with any vegetable dish or eggs.

PRIZE
OLD-FASHIONED PLUM PUDDING HARD SAUCE

2/3 cup butter	1/2 cup brandy
2 cups powdered sugar, sifted	2 teaspoons cream
Pinch of salt	1/2 cup almonds, chopped fine

Put the butter, powdered sugar, and salt into a wooden beat it to a light smooth creamy mixture. Gradually stir in the brandy. Harshly beat in the cream. Lastly stir in the nuts. Press this mixture evenly into a pan and set on ice until it hardens. Then cut into any desired shapes and serve with the pudding.

ORANGE HARD SAUCE IN THE OLDEN DAYS

1/4 cup butter	Pinch of salt
1 cup powdered sugar,	1 teaspoon orange rind,

sifted   grated
1 teaspoon water, boiling   1 tablespoon orange juice

Put the butter and sugar into a wooden mixing bowl and beat it to a light smooth creamy mixture. Gradually stir in the boiling water. Then stir in the salt, orange rind, and orange juice. Beat the mixture until it is fluffy. Serve immediately with any type pudding[7] or cake.[8]

CAULIFLOWER GRAVY FAVORITE
OF JOHN PAUL JONES

1 head cauliflower,   3 tablespoons butter
   small   Salt to taste
1 onion, small   Pepper to taste
1 bunch celery, small   Mace to taste
3/4 cup cream

Put the head of cauliflower into a saucepan and cover with salted water. Bring to a boil and cook until about half done. Then change the water and throw it away. Cook until tender in the fresh salted water. When done, save 3/4 cup of the cooking water when the cauliflower is drained. Mince the cauliflower and set it aside. Now put the onion and celery in another saucepan and cover with water. Boil them until tender. When done, drain and then mince them together.

Now put the 3/4 cup of cauliflower water into a saucepan and heat it. Stir in the cream. When warm add the cauliflower, onion, and celery. Chop up the butter and roll the bits in flour. Add this and the seasonings to the mixture. Bring to a quick boil and let it simmer until thick.

7. Recipes in Chapter 14.
8. Recipes in Chapter 13.

Serve immediately. *Note*: John Paul Jones developed a taste for this delicious gravy while engaged in the African slave trade between 1766 and 1767, under his real name of John Paul. He assumed the name *Jones* when later relocating in Virginia. This man became well known as an American naval officer at the outbreak of the Revolutionary War. He later saw service as a rear admiral in the Russian navy of 1788.

EARLY NEW ENGLAND FOAMY PUDDING SAUCE

2 tablespoons butter
1 cup powdered sugar
2 egg whites

1/2 cup water, boiling
1 teaspoon vanilla

Put the butter and powdered sugar into the top of a double boiler and beat until creamy. Whip in the egg whites, 1 at a time. Continue beating hard until the ingredients are fluffy and light. Then stir in the boiling water and beat until the mixture is foamy. Lightly stir in the vanilla and serve at once while hot.

WHITE CELERY GRAVY BEFORE THE CIVIL WAR

2 bunches celery, large
3/4 cup vegetable stock[9]
1 1/2 tablespoons flour
1 1/2 tablespoons butter

Salt to taste
Pepper to taste
Nutmeg to taste
3/4 cup cream
or
3/4 cup milk

Put the celery into a saucepan and cover with boiling

9. Recipe in Chapter 5.

water. Simmer it until tender. Then drain and cut into bits 1/2 inch long. Now put the vegetable stock into a saucepan and warm it. Thicken with flour. Stir in the butter and seasonings. Lastly stir in the cream or milk. Beat until smooth. Put in the celery chunks and bring to almost a boil. Stir continuously. Serve in a tureen[10] or, if preferred, pour it directly over the vegetables.

OLD-FASHIONED WHOLE CRANBERRY SAUCE

2 cups cranberries, fresh	2 cups water
	2 cups sugar

Blend the cranberries, water, and sugar in a saucepan. Bring to a boil and then let the mixture simmer for 5 minutes, or until the cranberries burst open. Stir continuously. Then take from the stove and pour into a serving bowl. Set aside to cool. *Note*: Whole cranberry sauce is even better if set on ice and chilled thoroughly before serving.

GREAT-GREAT-GRANDMOTHER HORTON'S DRAWN BUTTER GRAVY

2 teaspoons flour	3/4 cup milk
Pinch of salt	2 tablespoons butter

Thoroughly blend the flour and salt in a wooden mixing bowl. Gradually add the milk. Beat until it is smooth and creamy. Put the mixture in a metal cup or small saucepan. Set it in a pan of boiling water. Stir continuously as it warms. When it has simmered for 2 minutes, add the butter by degrees. Stir all the time until the butter is entirely

---

10. Table dish for gravy.

melted and incorporated with the flour and water. Boil for 1 minute and then serve while hot.

or

1 teaspoon flour, heaping	1 egg, well beaten
1 cup water, hot	3 tablespoons butter, well rounded

Wet the flour to a smooth paste with a little cold milk or water. Put the hot water in a small saucepan and set it in a larger pan of boiling water. Then blend the flour with the water in the saucepan and stir until it thickens. Take out 3 teaspoons of this hot mixture and whip each, 1 at a time, into the frothy beaten egg. Then set this aside.

Stir the butter into the balance of the contents in the saucepan. When the butter is melted and thoroughly blended, take the beaten egg mixture and gradually stir it into the saucepan mixture. Beat hard and serve immediately.

VICKSBURG'S
FAMED OLD-TIME LEMON HARD SAUCE

1/3 cup butter	Pinch of salt
4 teaspoons lemon juice	1 1/4 cups powdered sugar
1/2 teaspoon lemon rind, grated	

Cream the butter in a wooden mixing bowl until it is soft and smooth. Stir in the lemon juice and grated rind. Beat in the salt and powdered sugar. Continue whipping until the mixture is creamy and stiff. Press the sauce into a cup or mold. Serve either chilled or as is. *Note*: This delightful sauce is wonderful with fruit cakes[11] or puddings.[12]

---

11. Recipes in *Natural Baking the Old Fashioned Way,* by the author.
12. Recipes in Chapter 14.

GREAT-GRANDMOTHER SHAW'S
OLD-FASHIONED ONION GRAVY

4 white onions,
   large
3/4 cup milk, hot

3 tablespoons butter
Salt to taste
Pepper to taste

Peel the onions and put them into a saucepan. Cover with salted water and boil them until tender. When done, drain and press all the water from them. Then mince the onions. Put the milk into a saucepan and bring it to a boil. Stir in the minced onions. Then add the butter and seasonings. Simmer for 2 minutes and serve while steaming hot.

MUSHROOM GRAVY FAVORITE OF AARON BURR

3/4 cup mushrooms
3/4 cup cream
   or
3/4 cup milk
4 tablespoons butter

1/4 teaspoon mace
1/4 teaspoon nutmeg
Salt to taste
1 teaspoon flour

Put the mushrooms into a saucepan and barely cover with water. When tender, drain, but do not press them. Add the cream or milk, butter, and seasonings. Simmer and stir continuously until the mixture begins to thicken. Then wet the flour in cold milk and stir it in. Bring to a quick boil and pour into a gravy boat. Serve while steaming hot. *Note*: Aaron Burr had an undying love for fresh mushrooms prepared in the above way. This is the man who was vice-president under Thomas Jefferson in 1801. He later killed Alexander Hamilton in an 1804 duel.

5

Sensational Old-time Natural Soups

GREAT-GRANDMOTHER'S
OLD-TIME SOUP POINTERS

In making a thickening for any soup, rub the butter and flour together. Then add to the hot liquid.

Cream soups are always in season and can be made using any type vegetables.

Vegetables that are extremely tough, and of little use in other cooking, may readily be used for soups. Never soak your vegetables because they lose nutrients.

Save all leftover vegetables. If there is a teaspoon of any type vegetable, a stalk of celery, an egg, a baked apple. or a bit of macaroni, put them neatly away for future use. All leftovers, even cheese, bread, and grains should be saved and eventually recycled as a soup ingredient.

If you boil any rice, cook vegetables, or even use a steamer with vegetables, always save the water and keep it in a sealed container. Refrigerate until needed for soups.

A puree is simply a soup that is made thicker than the regular cream soup. It is nourishing and delicious when properly prepared.

71

A little whipped cream dropped into each bowl of soup as it is served will add much to its flavor.

Fruit soups are always popular during hot weather. They are wholesome and delicious. Any type fruit juice may be thickened with cornstarch or arrowroot starch. It can be made with or without the addition of fresh fruit. And it can be suitably served while hot or cold.

NATURAL VEGETABLE SOUP STOCK
IN EARLY AMERICA

A great variety of vegetables can be used in making good soup stock. Cut some turnips, carrots, celery, and onions and put them into a tightly covered kettle of cold water. A quart of water is the usual allowance for every pound of vegetables. Let them soak for 1 hour. Then simmer, but not boil, for several hours. This will draw out the nutrients and flavor of each individual vegetable.

If you have any water from previously cooked rice or vegetables, use it instead of fresh water from the tap. And toss in any vegetable remnants or leftovers from the refrigerator.

When the vegetables have been simmered until they are done, drain off the water and add an equal amount of rich bean broth. Then add a little wheat flour, celery flakes or seeds, butter, and a small amount of strained tomato to kill the sweet vegetable flavor. This stock should be the consistency of broth when it is finished. If thicker than broth, it should be diluted with water when used as a basis for any kind of soup.

OLD-FASHIONED CREAM SOUP POINTERS

Rub 1 heaping tablespoon butter with 2 tablespoons sifted flour until it is smooth and creamy. Then slowly melt it in a saucepan over the fire. When melted, add 4 cups milk (when available). Stir constantly. When this thickens, add a little salt, and whatever herbal seasonings are desired. Lastly add the ingredients you want in the soup itself.

VEGETABLE BOUILLON
IN THE LONG-FORGOTTEN PAST

This is simply vegetable soup stock with water added to reduce it to the desired strength. It is to be served in cups. A special vegetable bouillon can be made as follows:

8 cups vegetable stock[1]	2 bay leaves
2 cups tomatoes, stewed and strained	1 tablespoon salt
	2 onions, grated

Blend all of the above ingredients in a kettle and let them stew for 3 hours. Then strain this mixture and put away until needed. Reheat before serving. This should cook down to about 1/2 its original quantity when done.

The Best of Old-Time Soups

HULLED CORN SOUP
FAVORITE OF RICHARD HENRY LEE

There is a distinctive flavor to hulled corn. It is especially agreeable to many, particularly those who have been accustomed to this dish in childhood, as was Lee. But often the corn is not quite tender enough. Or one wishes to serve it in a more modern way. Nevertheless, a soup or

---

1. Recipe included herein.

puree of this type will be found to be both novel and delicious. If the corn is tender, mash it until fine and sift through a puree strainer. Otherwise chop the corn fine before sifting. Then gradually stir in hot milk, enough to make it the consistency of any cream vegetable soup. Put it on to boil and add salt and pepper to taste. Add 1 generous tablespoon of butter for each 4 cups of the mixture. Serve with croutons.

This delightful soup will have a slightly granular texture. If this is disliked, you may add the usual flour thickening —1 tablespoon butter and 1 tablespoon flour, blended together and stirred into the hot soup. If a corn puree is desired, simply mash and sift the corn. Then heat and season to taste with butter, salt, and pepper. Serve as a vegetable, or as a garnish for a main dish.

Note: Richard Henry Lee (1756–1818) enjoyed this soup best when it was made very simple and grainy. He was a general during the Revolutionary War and was best known as "Lighthorse Harry." Lee served as governor of Virginia from 1792 to 1795. He was a close personal friend of George Washington. Lee delivered the funeral oration when Washington died. It contained the now famous words: "First in war, first in peace, first in the hearts of his countrymen."

EARLY AMERICAN GREEN PEAS SOUP

12 cups vegetable stock[2]	4 cups green peas, uncooked
3/4 cup flour	Salt to taste

Make a thickening of 4 cups stock and the flour. Stir this into the other 8 cups stock as it boils. Add salt to taste (many old-timers liked to add a pinch of sugar as well). Then stir in the uncooked peas. Keep stirring until the soup

2. Recipe included herein.

mixture comes to a boil. Let it simmer until the peas are tender and done. Take care not to let it burn or scorch. Add butter or cream to enrich it if desired. Colonists usually preferred cream when it was available to them. Serve while steaming hot.

OLD PLANTATION TOMATO SOUP

4 cups tomatoes, stewed and strained	1 tablespoon butter
1 tablespoon onion, minced	1 tablespoon honey
1 tablespoon parsley flakes	1 teaspoon salt
	1/2 teaspoon pepper
	1 tablespoon flour

The use of vegetable stock in making tomato soup is not absolutely essential, as an excellent-tasting soup can be made with the above ingredients. Put the stewed tomatoes into a kettle with 2 cups hot water. Set aside until you fry the onion and parsley in the butter. When the onion has browned, stir in the honey, salt, and pepper. Lastly stir in the flour and blend until smooth. Turn all of this into the kettle of tomatoes. Let it simmer for 10 minutes. Serve while hot. *Note*: If vegetable stock is used, omit the hot water and butter. The flavor of onion may be objectionable, and the use of it is optional.

GREAT-GRANDMOTHER MITCHELL'S PEA-TOMATO SOUP

This delicious soup may be made with fresh vegetables or with the home-canned variety. The ingredients are as follows:

4 cups peas	3 tablespoons butter
2 1/2 cups tomatoes	3 tablespoons flour
10 peppercorns	1/4 teaspoon baking soda
2 onion slices	Salt to taste
Small bay leaf	Pepper to taste

Rinse the peas (if fresh) in cold water. Then put them into a kettle with 3 cups boiling water. Add the tomatoes, peppercorns, onion, and bay leaf. Boil for 20 minutes. When done rub the soup mixture through a strainer. Set aside while the butter and flour are blended to a creamy mixture in a small bowl. Add this to the soup as a thickening. Now stir in the baking soda. Season with salt and pepper to taste. A little sugar can be added if liked. Strain again and serve with croutons. *Note*: The croutons are made by buttering stale slices of bread, cutting them into small cubes, and crisping in a moderate oven (350 degrees).

BREAD SOUP
ON THE CONFEDERATE BATTLEFIELDS

This economical and nourishing soup may be made quickly, and it is an excellent way to dispose of stale bread crusts. Take 1 1/2 pounds of stale homemade bread[3] crusts and put them into 6 cups vegetable stock.[4] Add 2 well-rounded tablespoons of butter. Boil together for 3/4 hour and then serve while hot. Be sure to stir well while it cooks.

SCHUYLER COLFAX'S
FAVORITE BLACK BEAN SOUP

2 cups black beans	1/2 teaspoon celery flakes
4 cups vegetable stock[5]	1/4 teaspoon curry

3. Recipes in *Natural Baking the Old Fashioned Way*, by the author.
4. Recipe included herein.
5. Ibid.

1 tablespoon butter
1 tablespoon flour
1/2 teaspoon cloves
1/2 teaspoon cinnamon

Salt to taste
Pepper to taste
Juice of 2 lemons

This is believed to be one of the best bean soups known in the long-forgotten past. It is made as follows: Put the beans into a kettle with 4 cups boiling water and simmer until they are soft. Then strain them into the vegetable stock and heat. Meanwhile blend the butter and flour in a small bowl until it is a smooth cream. Then add this to the soup, and stir in all the seasonings. The lemon juice is to be blended just before serving. *Note*: And who was Schuyler Colfax? This forgotten American was the vice-president under Grant between 1869 and 1877.

CREAM OF CELERY SOUP IN EARLY NEW ENGLAND

1 bunch celery
1 tablespoon butter
1 tablespoon flour

2 cups milk, hot
Salt to taste
Pepper to taste

Wash and cut the celery stalks into 1-inch pieces. Put them into a kettle with 2 cups salted boiling water and cook until tender enough to mash. Strain through a colander. Then blend the butter and flour in a small bowl until creamy and smooth. Stir this into the hot milk. Then blend the hot milk with the strained celery. Salt and pepper to taste. Simmer this mixture for 5 full minutes. Then serve immediately. *Note*: A few drops of onion juice improves the flavor of this soup for some people. A good and easy way to get fresh onion juice is to rub the onion, after the outside skin has been removed, on a rough grater. 4 to 8 drops gives a suggestion, without the positive onion flavor.

EARLY MOBILE JULIENNE SOUP

Cut up some mixed vegetables—celery, turnip, and carrot—into small pieces. Bring 4 cups vegetable stock[6] to a boil. Put in the vegetables and cook until soft. Other in-season vegetables may also be used in this soup. Try asparagus, peas, and stringbeans. Season with salt and pepper to taste.

GREAT-GREAT-GRANDMOTHER HORTON'S CREAMED PEA SOUP

1/2 peck green peas	1 tablespoon butter
6 cups milk	1 tablespoon flour
1 egg, well beaten	

Shell the peas and put the pods into a large kettle with plenty of cold water. Set the fire and boil until the pods are tender. Drain and return the water to the kettle. Put in the fresh peas and again bring to a boil. Allow to cook for 1/2 hour. Take out 2 cups of the peas and set them aside. Mash the remaining peas in the kettle broth (water). Now add the milk and the whole peas to the kettle broth. Let it simmer for 3 minutes. Meanwhile take the frothy beaten egg, butter, and flour and blend them together in a wooden mixing bowl. When smooth and creamy, gradually mix this into the soup. Take from the stove and season with salt and pepper to taste. Serve immediately.

ORIGINAL OLD-TIME MOCK BISQUE SOUP

4 cups fresh tomatoes, mashed	3 tablespoons butter
1 tablespoon flour	4 cups milk

---

6. Recipe included herein.

Put the tomatoes into a kettle with a little water and stew them until they are soft. If very acid, use 1/2 teaspoon baking soda with them. Meanwhile blend the flour and butter in a wooden mixing bowl. When smooth and creamy, gradually stir the milk in. Put the hot tomatoes into the thickened milk mixture and season to taste with salt and pepper. Serve while very hot.

COLONIAL-STYLE TASTY FRESH CORN SOUP

This wonderful old-fashioned soup may be made with either fresh sweet corn or home-canned corn. It is preferable to use fresh corn. Cut and scrape the corn from the cob. For every cup of corn allow 2 cups cold water. Put the corn and water into a kettle and boil for 1 hour. Then press through a colander. For each cup corn you will need the following:

1 tablespoon butter, melted	Red pepper to taste
	2 cups milk, hot
1 tablespoon flour	1 cup cream, hot
Salt to taste	

Blend the melted butter and flour in a saucepan until it is a smooth creamy mixture. Season lightly with salt and red pepper. Pour this into the hot corn. Then add the hot milk and cream. Stir well and let stand for a few minutes before serving. Do not boil this again after the milk and cream have been added.

MRS. BOOTH'S HOMEMADE VEGETABLE SOUP

1 onion, sliced	1 turnip, diced
1/2 cup butter	1 large potato, diced

1 tablespoon flour	1 head cabbage, diced
4 cups vegetable stock[7]	Salt to taste
1 carrot, diced	Pepper to taste
1 parsnip, diced	

Put the onion and the butter into a frying pan and cook together until the onion has browned lightly. Gradually stir in the flour to thicken the mixture. When well blended, pour in the hot vegetable stock. Add all the vegetables. Other fresh vegetables may be added if desired, but Mrs. Booth's original recipe calls only for those listed above. Season to taste with salt and pepper. Simmer until all the vegetables are nice and tender. Add more hot stock if necessary. *Note*: Mrs. Booth made this exact same soup for her infamous son, John Wilkes Booth (1839–65), when he was a child. To avenge the defeat of the Confederacy Booth formed a conspiracy to assassinate Lincoln. He mortally wounded the president at Ford's Theater on April 14, 1865.

Early American Natural Soup Additions

DUMPLINGS
DURING THE REVOLUTIONARY WAR ERA

| 3 large fresh eggs, well beaten | 1 1/2 cups milk |
| | Flour to suit |

Blend the frothy beaten eggs and the milk together in a large wooden mixing bowl. Stir in sufficient flour to make a thick rich batter. This batter should be beaten until it is completely free from lumps. It is to be dropped into the boiling soup, a tablespoon at a time.

---

7. Recipe included herein.

GREAT-GREAT-GRANDMOTHER HORTON'S OLD-TIME EGG BALLS

9 egg yolks, hard-boiled   3 egg yolks, raw
1 tablespoon flour   1 1/2 teaspoons salt

Blend the hard-boiled egg yolks with the flour until it becomes a smooth creamy paste. Then beat in the raw egg yolks and the salt. When thoroughly mixed, form into small balls Drop the egg balls into the hot soup just before serving.

GREAT-GRANDMOTHER SHAW'S HOMEMADE NOODLES

2 large fresh eggs,   Pinch of salt
   well beaten   Flour to suit

Put the frothy beaten eggs into a wooden mixing bowl. Add the salt and sufficient flour to make a stiff dough. Put the dough on a floured board (or countertop) and roll it out in a 1/8-inch- to 1/4-inch-thick sheet. Sprinkle with more flour to keep it from sticking together. Roll the dough up into a scroll and slice it into strawlike strips. After cutting the dough, mix the strips lightly in flour. Drop them into the hot soup a few minutes before it is served. *Note*: These noodles must not be put into the soup while it is still boiling or they will fall apart from overcooking.

6

Fabulous Salads with Natural Foods

To make a perfect salad, there should be a miser for oil,
a spendthrift for vinegar, a wise man for salt, and a madcap
to stir the ingredients up and mix them well together.
                                        —An old Spanish proverb.

THE ORIGINAL 1893 WALDORF SALAD

Great-great-grandmother Horton's ordinary old-fashioned "Apple Salad" suddenly gained fame at the opening of the Waldorf Astoria Hotel in New York City. In March, 1893, at 5th Avenue and 33rd Street, site of William Waldorf Astor's imposing mansion, the famous hotel first opened its doors to the public. The hotel's maitre d', a close friend of my great-grandmother Sarah (Horton) Mitchell (1846-1929), introduced her mother's "Apple Salad" as the "Waldorf Salad." He later became world renowned as "Oscar of the Waldorf." It goes without saying that the "new" salad was an instant success with New York's notables of society. Today the hotel still lists "Waldorf Salad" on its menus, and there is a slightly revised, more modern version of the original recipe in the current *Waldorf Astoria Cookbook.*

It is still widely claimed that there is no original written recipe for the salad, yet the recipe was given to Oscar by Mrs. Mitchell, who in turn received it from her mother, Huldah (Radike) Horton. This "Apple Salad" was in fact served to General Lafayette on his visit to my great-great-grandmother Horton's home while in Newburgh, New York in 1824. The secret of the original recipe was undoubtedly the special old-fashioned homemade mayonnaise concocted by Mrs. Horton and also handed down to her daughter. And here is the authentic "Apple Salad" or "Waldorf Salad" recipe of the long-forgotten past:

2 1/2 cups celery, diced	16 lettuce leaves, fresh and large
2 1/2 cups apples, tart and diced	6 tablespoons walnuts, chopped
1 1/ cups mayonnaise[1]	

Thoroughly blend the celery, apples, and mayonnaise in a large wooden mixing bowl. Set on ice to thoroughly chill. Then place 2 crisp lettuce leaves on each salad plate. Put equal portions of the ice-cold salad mixture in the center of the lettuce leaves. Sprinkle liberally with walnuts over each dish of salad and serve immediately. *Note*: This makes 8 nice-sized portions. Great-great-grandmother Horton also blended the mayonnaise and walnuts together before adding the celery and apples. This made a pleasing variation.

EARLY NEW ENGLAND SUMMER SALAD

3 eggs, hardboiled	3 heads fresh lettuce
2 teaspoons sugar	5 tender radishes

---

1. Recipes in *Natural Cooking the Old Fashioned Way*, by the author.

1 teaspoon salt	1 cucumber
1 teaspoon pepper	2 teaspoons mustard
1 teaspoon made mustard[2]	leaves
2 tablespoons olive oil	Handful of watercress
3/4 cup cider vinegar[3]	

Rub the egg yolks to a smooth paste in a small wooden mixing bowl. Stir in the sugar, salt, pepper, mustard, and olive oil. Let it stand for 5 minutes. Then harshly beat in the cider vinegar. Set aside while the salad is being prepared. Cut up the lettuce, radishes, and cucumber, into very small pieces. Chop up the mustard leaves and watercress. Put all of these into a large wooden mixing bowl. Pour the previously made dressing over this. Toss very lightly so as not to bruise the tender vegetables. Heap in a salad bowl over a large lump of ice. Garnish with nasturtium blossoms and serve immediately.

GREAT-GREAT-GRANDMOTHER NORTHRUP'S LETTUCE SALAD

2 eggs, hardboiled	mustard[4]
1 teaspoon sugar	2 teaspoons olive oil
1 teaspoon pepper	4 tablespoons vinegar[5]
1/2 teaspoon salt	3 heads lettuce, large
1/2 teaspoon made	

Put the hard-boiled egg yolks into a wooden mixing bowl and rub them to a smooth creamy paste. Blend in the sugar, pepper, salt, mustard, and olive oil. Set aside and let

---

2. Recipes in *Natural Cooking the Old Fashioned Way*, by the author.
3. Ibid.
4. Ibid.
5. Ibid.

it stand for 5 minutes. Then beat in the vinegar. Meanwhile, cut the lettuce up with a knife and fork. Do not use a chopper or it will bruise. Put into a salad bowl and pour in the previously made salad dressing. Mix thoroughly by tossing the salad with a fork. *Note*: A popular old-fashioned method of eating this salad was to simply place the lettuce heads in a bowl on the table. The dressing was served in another bowl by itself, or olive oil and vinegar were blended instead. The lettuce was passed around and each person would pull off the desired amount of lettuce with their fingers. It was then sprinkled with the oil-vinegar mixture and seasoned to taste with salt and pepper.

OLD-FASHIONED RAW TOMATO SALAD

Do not loosen the tomato skins with scalding water. It impairs the flavor and destroys the crispness. Pare them with a sharp knife. Then slice and lay each piece in a glass dish. Season with a mixture of salt, pepper, and vinegar.[6] Stir a piece of ice rapidly around in the dressing before pouring it over the tomatoes. *Note*: According to my great-great-grandmother, "there is no salad, excepting, perhaps, lettuce and cucumbers, that is more improved by the use of ice than tomatoes."

AMBROSIA SALAD IN THE OLD SOUTH

8 sweet oranges, peeled and sliced	1/2 coconut, grated 1/2 cup powdered sugar

Arrange some of the orange slices in a glass serving dish. Scatter some of the grated coconut over the orange

6. Recipes in *Natural Cooking the Old Fashioned Way*, by the author.

slices. Sprinkle lightly with powdered sugar. Then cover this with another layer of orange slices. Fill up the dish in this sequence. Use coconut and powdered sugar for the last or top layer. Serve at once.

ANTHONY WAYNE'S FAVORITE CHEESE SALAD

1 egg, hard-boiled	1 teaspoon sugar
1 tablespoon olive oil	1 teaspoon made mustard[7]
1 teaspoon salt	1/2 pound old cheese, grated
1 teaspoon red pepper	1 tablespoon onion vinegar[8]

Put the egg yolk in a small bowl and add the olive oil. Rub together until they become a smooth creamy paste. Stir in the salt, pepper, sugar, and mustard. Lastly blend in the cheese. Beat all together well before adding the onion vinegar. Serve in a crab shell. This mixture bears a marvelous resemblance in taste to deviled crab. It makes a good impromptu relish at a tea or luncheon. It is delightful when eaten with homemade crackers[9] and butter. *Note*: Use none but the best and freshest olive oil in compounding this salad. If you can not obtain this, or are out of it, melted butter is the best substitute I know of. General Anthony Wayne (1745–96) was quoted as saying he never tired of this "cheese salad." He was a famous commander during the Revolutionary War who raised a volunteer regiment in 1776. This man was the hero of the storming and capture of Stony Point on July 15, 1779. He became known as "Mad Anthony," and stopped the Indian uprisings in the West of 1794 and 1795.

---

7. Recipes in *Natural Cooking the Old Fashioned Way*, by the author.
8. Ibid.
9. Recipes in *Natural Baking the Old Fashioned Way*, by the author.

PRIZE OLD-TIME
CRANBERRY-VEGETABLE SALAD

1 cup peas, cooked[10]	1 cup cranberries, cooked
1 cup carrots, cut in strips	Lettuce leaves
1 cup celery, diced	Salad dressing[11]

Blend the peas, carrots, and celery in a wooden mixing bowl. Split the cranberries in half and add these to the mixture. Thoroughly chill and then pile it on individual lettuce leaves. Add the salad dressing of your choice. Or it may be served with good old-fashioned homemade mayonnaise.[12]

GREAT-GRANDMOTHER MITCHELL'S
RAW CUCUMBER SALAD

Pare the cucumbers neatly from end to end. Lay them in icewater for 1 hour. Then wipe them and slice thin. Put the slices in a glass dish with some thin slices of onion. Season with a mixture of salt, pepper, and vinegar.[13] Use a little olive oil if you wish. Lay some bits of ice among the slices and serve immediately. *Note:* According to Great-grandmother Mitchell, "Cucumbers should be gathered while the dew is on them, and eaten the very same day." Always leave cucumbers in a cool place until you are ready to pare them.

SIMPLE POTATO SALAD IN COLONIAL TIMES

Cut some cold boiled potatoes into thin slices or small

10. Recipe in Chapter 3.
11. Recipes in Chapter 7.
12. Recipe in *Natural Cooking the Old Fashioned Way*, by the author.
13. Ibid.

chunks. Make a dressing by blending equal parts of olive oil and vinegar.[14] Add a pinch of red pepper, a pinch of salt, and 4 drops onion juice. Pour this over the potato slices. Mix carefully to avoid breaking the slices, or mashing the chunks. The garnish for this salad depends entirely upon the taste of the individual. Some old-timers used chopped beets, carrots, or parsley—or a combination of all three. Grated cheese was the preference of many people. *Note*: Chopped onion may be used instead of onion juice if a more pronounced flavor of onion is desired. And for a real treat, make this using the special potato salad dressing in chapter 7.

ISRAEL PUTNAM'S FAVORITE TOMATO SALAD

12 medium-sized tomatoes, peeled and sliced
4 eggs, hard-boiled
1 teaspoon salt
1/2 teaspoon red pepper
1 teaspoon sugar

2 teaspoons made mustard[15]
1 tablespoon olive oil
1 egg, well beaten
3/4 cup cider vinegar[16]

Put the slices of tomato on a large dish and set them on ice to chill while the dressing is being made. Then prepare the dressing as follows: rub the egg yolks to a smooth paste in a wooden mixing bowl. Add, by degrees, the salt, red pepper, sugar, mustard, and olive oil. Then whip in the frothy beaten egg. Lastly add the vinegar and blend well. Stir a great lump of ice rapidly in this dressing until it is cold. Take out the ice and cover the tomatoes with the mixture. Set it back on ice until it is sent to the table. This

---

14. Recipes in *Natural Cooking the Old Fashioned Way*, by the author.
15. Ibid.
16. Ibid.

salad is delicious, especially when it is properly mixed and chilled. *Note*: General Israel Putnam (1718-90) thoroughly enjoyed this identical salad at every opportunity. This American patriot was in charge of defending Philadelphia during the Revolutionary War. He was also a prominent leader at the battle of Bunker Hill in 1775. Putnam's mother was said to have first concocted this delightfully simple but tasty salad treat.

EARLY AMERICAN MACEDOINE SALAD

Any mixture of vegetables may be used for this salad. Peas, string beans, small bunches of cauliflower, beets, white turnips, and carrots give a pleasing variation in coloring. The vegetables should be cooked separately in boiling salted water. And as soon as the vegetables are done they should be transferred to ice water for at least 10 minutes. This enhances their brilliancy of coloring. If fancy cutters are used for those vegetables which require cutting it will add much to the attractiveness of the dish. Equal quantities of each vegetable should be utilized. Mix them together well and then marinate with a good French dressing.[17] They may then be arranged in a border of lettuce or other greens.

GREAT-GREAT-GRANDMOTHER DANIELS'S CELERY SALAD

6 stalks celery, cut into 1/2-inch bits	1 teaspoon sugar
	1 teaspoon made mustard[18]
1 egg, hard-boiled	1 tablespoon olive oil
Pinch of salt	1 egg, well beaten
Pinch of pepper	4 tablespoons vinegar[19]

17. Recipe in Chapter 7.
18. Recipes in *Natural Cooking the Old Fashioned Way*, by the author.
19. Ibid.

Put the celery chunks into a wooden mixing bowl and set them on ice while the special dressing is being made. Then prepare the dressing as follows: rub the egg yolk to a smooth paste. Add, by degrees, the salt, pepper, sugar, mustard, and olive oil. Then stir in the frothy beaten egg. Whip well and lastly stir in the vinegar. Put in a large lump of ice until the dressing becomes very cold. Take out the ice and pour the mixture over the chilled celery. Serve and eat at once as the vinegar will injure the crispness of the celery.

OLD NEW ORLEANS COLD SLAW

1/2 head cabbage chopped fine
1 cup vinegar[20]
2 tablespoons sugar

Salt to taste
Pepper to taste
1 tablespoon butter
1 egg, well beaten

Put the cabbage into a large wooden mixing bowl and set aside while preparing the following dressing: blend the vinegar, sugar, salt, pepper, and butter in a saucepan. Heat thoroughly but *do not* boil. Just before it scalds stir in the frothy beaten egg. Pour while hot, over the chopped cabbage in the bowl. Let it stand on ice and chill for a few minutes before serving.

OLD NEW ORLEANS HOT SLAW

1 head cabbage, sliced fine
1/2 cup water, hot
1 teaspoon salt

1 tablespoon butter
1 egg, well beaten
2 tablespoons vinegar[21]

20. Recipes in *Natural Cooking the Old Fashioned Way*, by the author.
21. Ibid.

Put the cabbage into a kettle and add the hot water. Cover the kettle closely and simmer for 30 minutes. Then stir in the salt, butter and frothy beaten egg. Blend thoroughly and then add the vinegar. Pour into a serving bowl and eat while hot.

GREAT-GRANDMOTHER SHAW'S
COLD CABBAGE SALAD

1 head cabbage, minced fine	2 teaspoons sugar
	1 teaspoon made mustard[22]
3 eggs, hard-boiled	2 tablespoons olive oil
1 teaspoon salt	3/4 cup vinegar[23]
1 teaspoon pepper	

Put the minced cabbage into a bowl and set aside on ice while the following dressing is being prepared: put the egg yolks into a small wooden bowl and rub them to a smooth creamy paste. Stir in the salt, pepper, sugar, mustard, and olive oil. Let it stand for 5 minutes. Then beat in the vinegar. Pour this mixture over the chilled cabbage and mix thoroughly by tossing it with a fork. Serve chilled.

HOT CABBAGE SALAD—A HOOD DELIGHT

1 cup vinegar[24]	1 tablespoon butter
Pinch of salt	1 head cabbage, shredded fine
Pinch of pepper	
1 tablespoon sugar	2 tablespoons sour cream

Blend the vinegar with all the ingredients for the dressing, except for the sour cream, in a saucepan. While it is

---

22. Recipes in *Natural Cooking the Old Fashioned Way*, by the author.
23. Ibid.
24. Ibid.

heating slowly, put the shredded cabbage into a large bowl. When the dressing comes to a boil, pour it over the cabbage. Set on ice until thoroughly chilled. Add the sour cream just before serving. Stir it in with a fork. *Note*: According to Mrs. Hood, "this is a very nice preparation of cabbage, and far more wholesome than the uncooked." It was her son's, General John Bell Hood's (1831–79), best-liked salad. He was the Confederate general who was soundly defeated by Sherman during the Siege of Atlanta from July 22 to September 2, 1864. His continued failures during the Civil War led to his being relieved of command in 1865.

7

Mouth-watering Old-time Natural Salad Dressings

DECATUR'S OWN BUTTERMILK SALAD DRESSING

3 egg yolks,
    well beaten
1 tablespoon butter,
    well rounded
1 teaspoon salt
2 teaspoons sugar

1/4 teaspoon dry mustard
2 teaspoons flour
Red pepper to taste
2 cups buttermilk
2 tablespoons vinegar[1]

Put the custardlike beaten egg yolks into a double boiler. Add the butter, salt, sugar, mustard, flour, and red pepper. Blend together well and then stir in the buttermilk and vinegar. Heat and stir continuously until it comes to a boil. Then set aside to cool. It will be ready to use when thoroughly cold. *Note*: This salad dressing is said to be the original creation of Stephen Decatur (1779–1820). He became famous in American naval history during the war with the Barbary States between 1801 and 1805. On February 16, 1804

---

1. Recipes in *Natural Cooking the Old Fashioned Way*, by the author.

his ship the *Enterprise*, burned Commander Bainbridge's *Philadelphia*, which had been captured the previous year.

OLD-FASHIONED THOUSAND ISLAND DRESSING

2 cups mayonnaise[2]
2 eggs, hard-boiled, chopped
1 green pepper, chopped fine
1 pimento, minced
2 tablespoons chives, chopped fine
1 cup chili sauce[3]
1 cup cream, whipped[4]

Blend the mayonnaise, eggs, green pepper, pimento, and chives in a wooden mixing bowl. Then whip in the chili sauce. Lastly fold in the thick and fluffy whipped cream. Chill well and then serve as needed. *Note*: This salad dressing can be placed in covered jars and kept cold until used.

GREAT-GREAT-GRANDMOTHER HORTON'S PINK DRESSING

1/2 cup strawberry juice
1/4 cup sugar
1/4 cup lemon juice
3/4 tablespoon butter
2 teaspoons corn starch

Put the fresh strawberry juice into a saucepan and add 1/2 the sugar to it. Set aside in a cool place for 2 hours. Then stir in the lemon juice and butter. Bring to a boil. Blend the rest of the sugar with the corn starch. Stir this into the hot saucepan mixture. Simmer for 3 minutes. Then let it cool and add it to your salad.

---

2. Recipes in *Natural Cooking the Old Fashioned Way*, by the author.
3. Ibid.
4. Ibid.

EARLY PHILADELPHIA SALAD DRESSING

6 egg yolks, well beaten
6 teaspoons sugar
3 teaspoons salt
1 teaspoon celery flakes
4 teaspoons dry mustard
1 teaspoon Worcestershire

sauce[5]
6 tablespoons olive oil
1 cup milk
1 teaspoon flour
1 cup vinegar,[6] hot

Put the custardlike beaten egg yolks into a double boiler. Blend in the sugar, salt, celery flakes, mustard, and Worcestershire sauce. Heat the mixture. Then gradually blend in the olive oil. Stir in the milk and flour. Lastly add the vinegar. Simmer carefully and stir continuously until the whole mixture is like a custard. Then pour into a covered bowl and allow to cool. It is then ready to use.

GREAT-GRANDMOTHER SHAW'S PLAIN SALAD DRESSING

3 tablespoons milk
1/4 tablespoon butter
1 egg yolk
1/4 teaspoon made
mustard[7]

1 teaspoon sugar
3 teaspoons vinegar[8]
Pinch of red pepper
1 egg white, stiffly beaten

Put the milk and butter into a double boiler and heat. Meanwhile blend together the egg yolk, mustard, sugar, vinegar, and red pepper. Stir this mixture into the hot milk-

---

5. Recipes in *Natural Cooking the Old Fashioned Way*, by the author.
6. Ibid.
7. Ibid.
8. Ibid.

butter mixture in the double boiler. Cook for 1 minute and then take from the fire. Lightly fold in the fluffy beaten egg white. Allow to cool and then serve.

SOUTHERN PLANTATION-STYLE BUTTER MAYONNAISE

3 egg yolks, well beaten	1 teaspoon salt
3 tablespoons butter, soft	1 teaspoon pepper
1 teaspoon dry mustard	1/3 cup vinegar[9]
1 teaspoon flour	1 cup cream, whipped

Blend the custardlike beaten egg yolks and the butter in a double boiler. Dissolve the mustard, flour, salt, and pepper in the vinegar. Beat this mixture into the egg-butter blend. Cook slowly and stir continuously until it thickens. Pour into a bowl and set aside to cool. When cold, fold in the whipped cream and serve.

SOUR CREAM FAVORITE OF ROBERT MORRIS

1 cup sour cream	Salt to taste
3 egg yolks, well beaten	Pepper to taste
1 teaspoon made mustard[10]	1/4 cup cider vinegar[11]
	1/2 tablespoon olive oil.

Put the sour cream into a double boiler and heat. When it comes to a boil pour *into* the custardlike beaten egg yolks. Stir in the mustard, salt, and pepper. Cook until it thickens. Stir frequently. Then take from the stove and set

9. Recipes in *Natural Cooking the Old Fashioned Way*, by the author.
10. Ibid.
11. Ibid.

aside to cool. When cold, stir in the cider vinegar and lastly the olive oil. *Note*: Fewer eggs can be used and cornstarch can be added to thicken this dressing. This particular salad dressing has great historical significance. It was a lifelong favorite of Robert Morris (1734-1806) who was known as the "Financier of the American Revolution." This man was a member of the Continental Congress in 1776 and one of the signers of the Declaration of Independence.

OLD-TIME ROQUEFORT CHEESE DRESSING

1/2 tablespoon salt	3/4 cup olive oil
1/2 teaspoon sugar	1 cup roquefort cheese,
1/3 cup lemon juice	mashed
1/2 teaspoon paprika	

Blend the salt, sugar, lemon juice, and paprika in a small mixing bowl. When well blended stir in the olive oil. Lastly whip in the mashed creamy cheese. Beat hard until smooth. *Note*: This is a delightful dressing for plain lettuce salad, or for use as desired on any other vegetable salad.

GREAT-GRANDMOTHER MITCHELL'S WHIPPED CREAM DRESSING

1 teaspoon salt	4 tablespoons lemon
1 teaspoon sugar	juice
5 egg yolks	1 cup cream
1/4 cup butter, melted	

Blend the salt, sugar, and egg yolks in a saucepan. Beat until it is custardlike in consistency. Then gradually add the melted butter and lemon juice. Set the saucepan in a larger pan of boiling water. Let it simmer until it thickens. Take from the stove and set aside to cool. While it is cooling, whip the cream until it is stiff and will stand by itself. Fold this carefully into the cold cooked mixture. Use on any type salad. It is absolutely delightful.

EARLY VIRGINIA SALAD DRESSING WITHOUT OIL

1 tablespoon vinegar[12]
1 egg yolk, well beaten
1/2 teaspoon dry mustard
1/2 teaspoon salt
1 teaspoon sugar

1/2 teaspoon butter
1 egg white stiffly
   beaten
Cream to suit

Put the vinegar into a saucepan with the custardlike beaten egg yolk. Heat and stir until it thickens. Then add the mustard, salt, sugar, and butter. Whip together well and allow it to cool to lukewarm. Then pour this into the fluffy beaten egg white. Stir lightly and add cream until the dressing is thin enough to pour and use.

GREAT-GREAT-GRANDMOTHER HORTON'S HONEY DRESSING

1 cup olive oil
3/4 cup cider vinegar[13]
   or
3/4 cup lemon juice
3/4 cup honey

1/2 teaspoon salt
1/2 teaspoon made
   mustard[14]
3/4 teaspoon celery seeds

Blend all of the above ingredients in a wooden mixing bowl. Beat together thoroughly. Then pour into small bot-

---

12. Recipes in *Natural Cooking the Old Fashioned Way*, by the author.
13. Ibid.
14. Ibid.

tles and seal. Store in a cool place until needed. Shake the bottle well each time before the dressing is used. *Note*: This recipe can be used as a tasty French dressing for all salads.

PRIZE EARLY AMERICAN DELUXE SALAD DRESSING

1/4 cup sugar	2 eggs, well beaten
1 1/2 teaspoons salt	1 cup sour cream
1 teaspoon dry mustard	1/2 cup vinegar[15]
1/4 teaspoon white pepper	

Thoroughly blend the sugar, salt, mustard, and white pepper. Put them in a double boiler. Then blend in the rest of the ingredients. Slowly cook until the mixture becomes thick and creamy. Pour into a bowl and set aside to cool. Use on all types salad.

MAGRUDER'S FAVORITE POTATO SALAD DRESSING

3 tablespoons sugar	1/2 teaspoon dry mustard
1 tablespoon flour	3 eggs, well beaten
1/2 teaspoon salt	3/4 cup vinegar,[16] warm
1/2 teaspoon pepper	Cream to suit

Blend the sugar, flour, salt, pepper, and mustard with the frothy beaten eggs. Stir this mixture into the warm vinegar. Beat hard until it thickens. Then set it aside to cool. When cold, add enough cream to thin the dressing down to a good pouring consistency. *Note*: This potato salad dressing was always preferred by Confederate General John Bankhead Magruder (1810–71). This man was victorious at Big Bethel, Virginia, on June 10, 1861. He has almost been forgotten with the passage of time.

---

15. Recipes in *Natural Cooking the Old Fashioned Way*, by the author.
16. Ibid.

8

Surprise Sandwich Fillings with Natural Foods

GREAT-GRANDMOTHER MITCHELL'S AVOCADO DELIGHTS

1 cup avocado, mashed   Pinch of salt
2 teaspoons lemon juice   Pinch of pepper
1/2 teaspoon onion juice   Pinch of paprika

Blend all of the above ingredients in a small wooden bowl. Spread on thin slices of fresh rye bread. Or spread it on crisp crackers for luncheons.

OLD-FASHIONED PEANUT SANDWICHES

Remove the skins from freshly roasted peanuts. Put the peanuts in a meat chopper and grind them to a paste. Spread a thick layer on unbuttered bread. Add a light sprinkle of salt before folding the slices together.

GREAT-GREAT-GRANDMOTHER HORTON'S EGG SANDWICH

12 eggs, hard-boiled	Salt to taste
1 1/4 cups walnuts chopped fine	Pepper to taste Salad dressing[1] to suit

Chop the egg whites up fine. Rub the yolks through a sieve. Then blend them together and add the walnuts, salt, and pepper. Add this mixture to any good salad dressing. Mix thoroughly and spread on fresh bread or crackers. Warm in the oven before serving. *Note*: This sandwich filling is wonderful when spread on hot, split homemade biscuits.[2] It is even better when blended with a little whipped cream along with the salad dressing.

EARLY AMERICAN CHEESE SPECIAL SANDWICH

1 cup cheese, grated	Salt to taste
1 tablespoon butter, melted	Pepper to taste

Blend the grated cheese and butter until it becomes a smooth paste mixture. Add salt and pepper to taste. Spread on fresh slices of bread.

PEMBERTON'S CUCUMBER SANDWICHES

1 large cucumber chopped	Salad dressing[3] to suit 1/2 cup walnuts,

---

1. Recipes in Chapter 7.
2. Recipes in *Natural Baking the Old Fashioned Way*, by the author.
3. Recipes in Chapter 7.

Quarter the cucumber and remove all the seeds. Chop it up fine. Drain and press for 1 hour. Now mix it with the walnuts. Add enough salad dressing to make a thick paste. Spread on thin slices of bread. *Note*: Many people thought General Pemberton's love for cucumber sandwiches was odd until they tasted one of his. He generally made them with homemade roquefort cheese dressing.[4] This Confederate officer defended Vicksburg against Grant's siege from May 18 to July 4, 1863. He was eventually defeated.

ORIGINAL OLD-TIME DATE SANDWICHES

16 dates, mashed   1/2 cup walnuts,
                                chopped fine

Spread thin slices of bread with butter. Blend the mashed dates and walnuts. Add a little cream if the mixture is too stiff to easily spread. *Note*: Mashed dates spread generously on unbuttered slices of bread also makes a delightful sandwich.

GREAT-GRANDMOTHER SHAW'S
CHEESE-NUT SANDWICHES

4 cups walnuts, chopped   Pinch of salt
4 cups cheese, grated   Cream to suit

Blend the nuts and cheese together and salt to taste. Then stir in enough heavy cream to make the mixture spread well. Spread thickly on fresh slices of bread or crackers. *Note*: A little whipped cream may be substituted in place of regular cream. Try it both ways.

---

4. Recipes in Chapter 7.

OLIVE SANDWICHES IN OLD NEW ENGLAND

1/2 cup almonds
1 cup green olives,
   chopped fine

1 tablespoon lemon juice
Salt to taste

Blanch the almonds in boiling water. Then toast them in a moderate oven (350 degrees) until a light brown. Chop them up fine and blend with the olives. Stir in the lemon juice. Salt to taste. Spread thickly on slices of bread.

DELIGHTFUL OLDEN-DAY JELLY SANDWICHES

Delicious yet simple sandwiches can be made by spreading slices of fresh bread with jelly.[5] Then sprinkle over the jelly with finely chopped nuts.

GREAT-GREAT-GRANDMOTHER DANIELS'S PRUNE SPECIALS

1/2 cup prunes, mashed
1 teaspoon lemon juice

1/2 cup nuts, chopped
2 drops almond extract

Blend all of the above ingredients in a wooden mixing bowl. Spread on thin slices of fresh cracked wheat or whole wheat bread. Or try this with fresh rye bread.

DELICIOUS OLD-FASHIONED SANDWICH FILLING IDEAS

Blend 1/2 cup cup chopped celery, 1/2 cup ground car-

5. Recipes in *Natural Cooking the Old Fashioned Way*, by the author.

rots, 1/2 cup chopped nuts, and enough mayonnaise[6] to make a spread.

Blend 1/2 cup chili sauce,[7] 1/2 cup chopped sweet pickle, [8] and 1 cup baked beans.

Blend 1/2 cup roquefort cheese, 1/4 cup finely chopped celery, and a dash of Worcestershire sauce.[9]

Blend 1 cup peanut butter, 1 cup finely chopped apple, and 1 teaspoon lemon juice.

Blend 1/2 cup shredded raw spinach, 1/2 cup celery, 2 chopped hard-boiled eggs, 1/2 chopped onion, and enough mayonnaise[10] to make a spread.

Blend 1/2 cup quince jelly and 1/2 cup chopped walnuts.

Blend 1/2 cup roquefort cheese, 1/4 cup finely chopped blanched almonds, and a dash of Worcestershire sauce.[11]

Blend 1 cup chopped figs, 1/2 cup chopped peanuts, and lemon juice to taste.

Blend 1 cup chopped cabbage, 1/2 cup chopped peanuts, and enough mayonnaise[12] to make a spread.

Blend 1/2 cup roquefort cheese, 1/4 cup chopped onion, 1/4 cup chopped celery, and cream enough to make a spread.

Blend 1/2 cup finely ground peanuts and enough salad dressing[13] to make a spread.

Blend 1/2 cup chopped water cress, 1/2 cup chopped cucumber, 2 tablespoons chives, and enough mayonnaise[14] to make a spread.

Blend 1/2 cup mashed bananas, 1 teaspoon lemon juice,

---

6. Recipes in *Natural Cooking the Old Fashioned Way*, by the author.
7. Ibid.
8. Ibid.
9. Ibid.
10. Ibid.
11. Ibid.
12. Ibid.
13. Recipes in Chapter 7.
14. Recipes in *Natural Cooking the Old Fashioned Way*, by the author.

and olive oil enough to make a spread. Or simply saturate thin slices of banana with lemon juice and olive oil.

Blend 1 cup peanut butter, 1/2 cup chopped raw spinach, and enough mayonnaise[15] to make a spread.

Blend 1 cup ground raw carrots, 1/2 cup chopped sweet pickle, and enough mayonnaise[16] to make a spread.

---

15. Recipes in *Natural Cooking the Old Fashioned Way,* by the author.
16. Ibid.

9

Wonderful Old-time Natural Fried Treats

EARLY AMERICAN FRITTER-MAKING TIPS

Have plenty of nice sweet shortening or butter in which to fry fritters. Test the heat by dropping in 1 teaspoon of the fritter mixture before risking more. If the butter or shortening is right, the batter will quickly rise to the surface in a puff-ball. The fritter will sputter and dance, and it will speedily assume a rich golden brown color. Take it out of the hot butter as soon as it is done. Use a skimmer for this purpose. Shake it to dislodge any drops of grease that may adhere to it. Drain on some brown paper. Then pile the fritters in a hot dish and send instantly to the table. Sprinkle powdered sugar on all except the vegetable fritters. Fry as many at a time as the kettle will hold. A round-bottomed saucepan or kettle, rather wide at the top, is always best for frying fritters.

MRS. GREENE'S GREEN CORN FRITTERS

2 cups green corn, grated	1 tablespoon cream or
3 eggs, well beaten	1 tablespoon milk

Salt to taste
1 tablespoon butter, melted

2 tablespoons flour

Stir the corn into the frothy beaten eggs by degrees. Beat together hard and then add salt to taste. Stir in the melted butter and then the cream or milk. Lastly thicken the mixture with the flour. This will help hold the batter together as it cooks. You may fry the fritters in deep hot butter, or cook them on a hot griddle, like batter cakes. Test a little first, to see that the batter is of the right consistency. *Note*: Eaten at breakfast or dinner, these fritters always seem to meet with a cordial welcome. Nathanael Greene's (1742–86) mother fixed this delightful dish for her son many times over the years. He was a noted soldier during the Revolutionary War who gained fame and served with great distinction at Trenton and other great battles. Greene was given an appointment as major-general on August 9, 1776.

PEA FRITTERS ON THE OLD PLANTATION

2 eggs, well beaten
1 cup milk
1/4 teaspoon baking soda

1/2 teaspoon cream of tartar
1/2 cup flour

Cook 3 more cups of peas than you need for dinner. Mash them while hot with a wooden spoon. Season with salt, pepper, and butter. Cover and set aside until morning. In the morning make a batter by combining the above ingredients. Stir the pea mixture into this and beat together very hard. Cook in deep fat, or on a hot griddle as you would ordinary pancakes. *Note*: I can testify, from experience, that this makes a wonderful accompaniment to any dinner, as well as a delightful breakfast dish.

GREAT-GREAT-GRANDMOTHER HORTON'S
JELLY FRITTERS

1 teaspoon cornstarch	2 tablespoons powdered
1 cup sponge cake[1]	sugar
crumbs, fine and dry	2 tablespoons currant jelly[2]
1 cup milk, boiling	or
4 egg yolks, well beaten	2 tablespoons cranberry jelly
	4 egg whites, stiffly beaten

Wet the cornstarch in a little cold milk. Soak the sponge cake crumbs in the boiling milk. Stir in the wet cornstarch. Bring this to a boil while continuously stirring. Set aside and let it cool a little. Then stir the custardlike egg yolks into this mixture. Blend in the sugar. Whip in the jelly, a little at a time. Then beat the entire mixture very hard. Lastly fold in the fluffy beaten egg whites. Deep fry immediately in large spoonfuls.

POPULAR COLONIAL ERA FRITTERS

2 cups flour	4 egg yolks, well beaten
1 teaspoon salt	4 egg whites, stiffly
2 cups water, boiling	beaten

Stir the flour and salt gradually into the boiling water. Whip hard while it boils for 3 minutes. Set aside and let it get almost cold. Then beat in the custardlike beaten egg yolks into this mixture. Lastly fold in the fluffy beaten egg whites. Beat the entire mixture very hard. Deep fry immediately, in large spoonfuls.

---

1. Recipes in *Natural Baking the Old Fashioned Way*, by the author.
2. Recipe in *Natural Cooking the Old Fashioned Way*, by the author.

APPLE FRITTERS—A FAVORITE OF SHERIDAN

1/4 cup brandy	1/2 teaspoon baking soda
1 tablespoon sugar	1 teaspoon cream of
1 teaspoon cinnamon	tartar
6 large apples,	3 cups flour
pared and quartered	Pinch of salt
4 cups milk	6 egg whites, stiffly
6 egg yolks, well beaten	beaten

Put the brandy, a very little water, the sugar, and cinnamon into a covered saucepan with the apples. Simmer and stir gently until about half done. Drain off every drop of the liquor. Set the apple pieces aside to cool.

or

You may simply parboil (partially cook) the apple pieces in clear water, with a very little sugar, and proceed as just directed above. Then make the batter as follows:

Stir the milk into the custardlike beaten egg yolks. Dissolve the baking soda in a little water and blend this into the egg-milk mixture. Then sift the cream of tartar with the flour. Gradually stir this into the mixture. Add the salt. Lastly whip in the fluffy beaten egg whites. Then put the cold mashed apples in the batter. Beat the entire mixture very hard. Deep fry at once, in large spoonfuls. *Note*: Philip Henry Sheridan (1831–88) was the Union general who defeated Lee at Five Forks, Virginia, April 1, 1865, and at Sailor's Creek on April 6, 1865. This notable leader often requested apple fritters with his meals. They were made exactly as above.

ORIGINAL PARSNIP FRITTERS IN THE COLONIES

3 large parsnips	1 cup cream

2 eggs, well beaten	or
1 tablespoon butter	1 cup milk
1 teaspoon salt	3 tablespoons flour

Put the parsnips into a kettle and cover them with water. Boil them until tender. Then drain and mash until they are smooth. Carefully pick out all the woody bits of fiber. Stir the mashed parsnips into the frothy beaten eggs. Whip hard while adding the butter and salt. Next stir in the cream or milk and lastly the flour. Fry as fritters in deep fat, or as cakes on a hot griddle.

GREAT-GRANDMOTHER MITCHELL'S BREAD FRITTERS

4 cups milk, boiling	1 tablespoon butter, melted
2 cups bread crumbs, fine and dry	Pinch of salt
	1 teaspoon nutmeg
3 egg yolks, well beaten	Pinch of baking soda
	3 egg whites, stiffly beaten

Put the boiling milk into a large wooden mixing bowl. Add the bread crumbs and cover. Leave to soak for 10 minutes. Then beat to a smooth paste. Stir in the custardlike beaten egg yolks, melted butter, salt, and nutmeg. Dissolve the baking soda in a little hot water and then add it to the mixture. Lastly whip in the fluffy beaten egg whites. Beat the entire mixture very hard. Deep fry at once in large spoonfuls.

OLD SOUTHERN FRUIT FRITTERS

1 cup cream	1/4 teaspoon salt
2 egg yolks	1 teaspoon baking powder

1 1/2 cups flour
1 tablespoon butter, melted

2 egg whites, stiffly beaten

The batter for all fruit fritters is essentially the same, and is made as follows: Stir the cream into the egg yolks. Blend the flour and melted butter in a wooden mixing bowl. Stir the egg-cream mixture into this. Beat very hard and then add the salt. When ready to use add the baking powder and the fluffy beaten egg whites. For banana fritters slice 8 bananas either lengthwise or across. Dip each piece in the batter. Deep fry in hot fat until browned. For pineapple fritters, pare and slice the pineapple several hours before it is to be used. Sprinkle with sugar. Dip in the batter and fry the same as the banana fritters.

GREAT-GRANDMOTHER SHAW'S JELLY CAKE FRITTERS

Cut some stale sponge cake,[3] or plain cup cakes[4] into 2- or 3-inch round pieces about 1/2 inch thick. Deep fry in hot butter or oil as you would any other fritters. When nicely browned take out of the oil and dip each piece in a bowl of boiling milk. Drain off the excess milk on the side of the bowl. Lay the cakes on a hot dish. Spread each one thickly with blackberry jam,[5] gooseberry jelly,[6] or some other delicate mixture. Pile them neatly on a serving dish and send around the table hot, with cream to pour over them. *Note*: This is a nice way of using up stale cake. Properly prepared, the dessert is almost equal to Neapolitan pudding.[7]

3. Recipes in *Natural Baking the Old Fashioned Way*, by the author.
4. Ibid.
5. Recipes in *Natural Cooking the Old Fashioned Way*, by the author.
6. Ibid.
7. Ibid.

EARLY NEW ENGLAND CELERY FRITTERS

1 egg yolk	2 teaspoons olive oil
3 tablespoons ice water	or
1/4 cup flour	2 teaspoons butter, melted
1/2 teaspoon salt	1 egg white, stiffly beaten
Pinch of pepper	Celery to suit

Beat the egg yolk with the ice water. Stir in the flour and beat again until it is smooth and creamy. Add the salt, pepper, and olive oil or melted butter. Beat hard again. Stir the fluffy beaten egg white into the batter. This should make it the consistency of a thick pour batter. Set aside for 3 hours. In the meantime cut the celery into 4-inch lengths. Drop into salted boiling water for 10 minutes. Drain and then dry each piece on a towel. Dip each stalk into the batter and drop into smoking hot deep fat. When golden brown, drain on unglazed paper and serve.

MRS. KING'S PLAIN OLD-FASHIONED FRITTERS

4 cups milk	1 teaspoon cream of tartar
6 egg yolks, well beaten	3 cups flour
	Pinch of salt
1/2 teaspoon baking soda	6 egg whites, stiffly beaten

Stir the milk into the custardlike beaten egg yolks. Dissolve the baking soda in a little water and blend this in with the milk-egg mixture. Then sift the cream of tartar with the flour. Gradually stir this into the mixture. Add the salt. Lastly whip in the fluffy beaten egg whites. Beat the entire batter very hard. Deep fry at once in great ladlefuls. *Note*: Mrs. King often prepared her fritters in the above

WONDERFUL FRIED TREATS 113

way for her husband William Rufus King. And who was this man? He was the vice-president of the United States under Franklin Pierce between 1853 and 1857.

CRANBERRY FRITTERS
IN EARLY NORTH CAROLINA

1 cup flour	2 tablespoons milk
1/4 teaspoon salt	1 egg, well beaten
1 1/2 teaspoons sugar	3/4 cup cranberry sauce
1 teaspoon baking powder	1/2 tablespoon lemon juice

Blend the flour, salt, sugar, and baking powder in a large wooden mixing bowl. Sift them all together. Stir the milk into the frothy beaten egg. Beat together and then add to the flour mixture. Beat this until smooth and creamy. Then add the cranberry sauce and lemon juice. Beat again, this time long and hard. Deep fry at once in large spoonfuls. Drain when done on brown paper. Sprinkle with powdered sugar and serve while hot. *Note*: These particular fritters are delicious when eaten with a good foamy sauce.[8]

8. Recipe in Chapter 4.

10

Tantalizing Drinks with Natural Foods

GREAT-GREAT-GRANDMOTHER DANIELS'S
PICNIC COFFEE

1 egg, well beaten	10 tablespoons fresh ground coffee

Use a plain, old-fashioned coffeepot. See that it is thoroughly cleansed. Stir the frothy beaten egg into the freshly ground coffee. Put the mixture into a cheesecloth bag. Place the bag into the coffee pot. Pour in 10 cups cold water. Place the cover on the pot. Allow the contents to come to a boil. Let it continue boiling for 10 minutes. The coffee will then be ready to serve.

EARLY AMERICAN WINE MADE FROM CRANBERRIES

2 quarts cranberries	4 cups water

Put the cranberries in a stone jar and mash them to a pulp. Add the water. Stir well and then let it stand for

2 full days. Strain into a large bowl through a double flannel bag. Then mash 2 more quarts of fresh cranberries in the same stone jar. Cover these with the strained liquid. Set aside to steep for 2 more days. Strain again as before. Then add:

2 cups sugar for each 3 quarts liquor

Blend in a kettle and bring to a boil. Let it simmer for 5 minutes. Put into a clean stone jar with a cloth thrown lightly over it. Set aside to ferment. When done working (fermenting), carefully skim off the top. Pour into sterilized bottles and seal until needed.

RASPBERRY VINEGAR—
A FAVORITE DRINK OF MEADE

Put as many raspberries as you wish into a stone jar and mash them to a pulp. Add enough cider vinegar[1] to cover them well. Stand the jar in the sun for 12 hours. Then leave it overnight in a cool place (a cellar if you have one). Stir occasionally but well during this time. Then strain into a large bowl through a double muslin or flannel bag. Put as many fresh berries into the jar as you took out. Pour the strained vinegar over them. Mash and set in the sun again for 1 day. Strain again as before. Put the liquor into a kettle and for each quart add the following:

2 cups water   6 1/2 cups sugar

Heat slowly and stir until the sugar has dissolved. Then bring to a boil for 3 minutes. Skim off the scum, remove from the stove, and strain once more. Bottle while warm and seal. *Note*: This is a very pleasant and most refreshing old-fashioned drink. It was the favorite of General George

1. Recipe in *Natural Cooking the Old Fashioned Way,* by the author.

Gordon Meade (1815–72), the Union officer who defeated Lee at the battle of Gettysburg in July of 1863. This is believed to have been the single most important battle of the Civil War.

GREAT-GRANDMOTHER SHAW'S GRAPE DRINK

3 cups grape juice	Pinch of ginger
2 cups water, boiling	1 teaspoon cinnamon
2 tablespoons sugar	3 tablespoons lemon juice

Blend the grape juice, water, sugar, and spices in a small saucepan. Heat slowly and stir until the sugar dissolves. When it simmers stir in the lemon juice. Serve immediately while hot.

OLD SOUTH CAROLINA STRAWBERRY WINE

3 quarts strawberries	4 cups water
2 cups sugar	

Mash and strain the juice from the strawberries. Then blend in the sugar and water. Stir well and put into a clean, sweet cask. Leave the bung out. Set aside to ferment. When the working (fermenting) ceases close the cask tightly. Or drain it off into sterilized bottles and seal. *Note*: My great-great-grandmother claimed that this wine, as simple as it may seem to prepare, is excellent.

GREAT-GREAT-GRANDMOTHER HORTON'S
STRAWBERRY SHERBET

4 cups strawberries	1 tablespoon orange flower
6 cups water	water
Juice of 1 lemon	1 1/2 cups sugar

The strawberries should be fresh and ripe. Crush them to a smooth paste. Stir in the lemon juice and orange flower water. Let it stand for 3 hours. Then strain through cheesecloth over the sugar. Squeeze the cloth hard. Stir until the sugar is all dissolved. Strain again and set on ice for at least 2 hours (longer if possible) before serving.

COLONIAL-STYLE EGG NOG SPECIAL

8 teaspoons honey	2 teaspoons vanilla
4 eggs, well beaten	Nutmeg to suit
4 cups cream, chilled	

Stir the honey into the frothy beaten eggs. Beat together until it becomes thick and custardlike. Then whip in the cream and vanilla. Set on ice and chill thoroughly. When ready to serve pour it into tall glasses. Sprinkle with nutmeg. This should always be served while very cold. *Note*: Almond or other flavoring extracts may be substituted for the vanilla if desired.

OLD-FASHIONED CREAMED TOMATO DRINK

6 stalks celery, grated	Salt to taste
1 1/2 cups cream, chilled	Red pepper to taste
3 cups tomato juice, chilled	1/3 cup ice, crushed
	3 drops onion juice

Combine all of the above ingredients in a large glass jar. Shake hard until thoroughly blended. Pour over more ice and immediately serve.

GREAT-GRANDMOTHER MITCHELL'S ELDERBERRY WINE

8 quarts elderberries	4 quarts water, boiling

Put the elderberries into a large porcelain kettle. Pour the boiling water over them. Let this stand for 12 hours. It should be stirred occasionally. Then strain well through a cheesecloth. Press all the juice out of the elderberries. For every 4 quarts of juice, add the following:

6 cups sugar   1/2 tablespoon cloves
1 tablespoon cinnamon

Bring to a boil and boil hard for 5 minutes. Pour this hot mixture into a stone jar, and throw a cloth lightly over it. Set aside to ferment. When it finishes working (fermenting) carefully remove the scum from the top of the liquid. Pour the wine into sterilized bottles and seal.

CIVIL WAR ERA ORANGE TEA

2 1/2 tablespoons   4 cups water, cold
  black tea leaves   4 whole cloves
4 cups water, boiling   Juice of 1/2 lemon
1 cup sugar   Juice of 3 oranges

Put the tea leaves into a saucepan with the boiling water. Let it steep for 5 minutes. Then strain. Put the sugar in another saucepan. Add the cold water and cloves. Bring to a boil and stir until the sugar all dissolves. Pour this syrupy mixture into the tea. Add the fruit juices last. Serve while steaming hot.

RASPBERRY ROYAL OF THE DALLAS FAMILY

4 cups ripe raspberries   2 cups sugar
4 cups cider vinegar[2]   2 cups brandy

2. Recipe in *Natural Cooking the Old Fashioned Way,* by the author.

Put the raspberries into a stone jar. Pour the cider vinegar over them. Add the sugar. Then pound the raspberries to a paste with a wooden pestle, or mash them with a wooden spoon. Let this stand in the sun for 4 hours. Then strain through cheesecloth. Squeeze out all of the juice. Blend the brandy with this strained berry juice. Pour into sterilized bottles and seal. Stir 2 tablespoons into a tumbler of ice water when you wish to drink this concoction. *Note:* This drink was a favorite of George M. Dallas whenever he was relaxing. This man was vice-president under President Polk between 1845 and 1849. He used to lay the bottles on their sides in his cellar. They were then covered with sawdust until needed.

OLD RHODE ISLAND CRANBERRY COCKTAIL

4 cups cranberries	2/3 cup sugar
4 cups water	

Put the cranberries and water into a large saucepan. Bring to a boil and then let simmer until all the berry skins pop open. This should take about 5 minutes. Then strain through cheesecloth. Put the juice back into the pan and bring it to a quick boil. Stir in the sugar and boil for 2 more minutes. Stir as it boils so as to dissolve the sugar. Set aside to cool. Then set it on ice to chill. Serve while very cold. *Note:* For future use put it into sterilized bottles and seal.

CAMBRIC TEA IN COLONIAL DAYS

1 tablespoon sugar	2 cups water, boiling
2 tablespoons cream	

Place the sugar and cream in a teapot. Fill with the boiling water and stir well. Serve in a teacup. *Note*: This makes an unusually good, easily digested old-fashioned tea drink. It was extremely popular during colonial times.

GREAT-GREAT-GRANDMOTHER NORTHRUP'S OLD-TIME TEA TIPS

To make excellent tea exactly as they used to do in the colonies, use 1/2 teaspoon tea for every cup water. Place the tea in an earthen dish. Pour in the desired quantity of boiling water. Cover tightly. Allow it to stand not less than 3 nor more than 7 minutes. Serve with cream, sugar, or thin slices of lemon and cloves. Old-timers claim that really good tea requires the water to have been freshly boiled.

11

Great Old-time Natural Bread, Rolls, and Muffins

GREAT-GREAT-GRANDMOTHER HORTON'S WHOLESOME BUTTERMILK BREAD

2 cups buttermilk	1 teaspoon baking powder
Flour to suit	Pinch of salt
1/4 cup yeast[1]	2 tablespoons butter, melted

Heat the buttermilk until it is scalding hot. Pour it into a large wooden mixing bowl. Stir in enough flour to make a tolerably thick batter. Add the yeast and stir well. Cover the bowl with a heavy towel and set aside in a warm place to rise for 5 hours. When the dough is light (has risen) dissolve the baking powder in a little hot water. Blend it, the salt, melted butter, and enough flour to enable you to handle the dough comfortably. Turn it out on a floured board (or countertop). Knead it well for at least 15 minutes. Form into loaves, cover with a towel, and let rise again until they are light. Then bake in a moderately quick

---

1. Recipes in *Natural Baking the Old Fashioned Way,* by the author.

oven (375 degrees). This makes a very white and whole-some bread. *Note*: If you are going to make this bread at night and leave it to bake in the morning, you do not need the yeast. Put in instead 1 tablespoon sugar.

ORIGINAL EARLY NEW ORLEANS BUTTER ROLLS

1/2 cake yeast	2 tablespoons sugar
1/4 cup water, lukewarm	1 teaspoon salt
2 cups milk, scalded	Flour to suit
1/2 cup butter	

Crumble and dissolve the yeast in the lukewarm water. Put the scalding milk into a large wooden mixing bowl. Blend in the butter, sugar, and salt. Set aside to cool. When the milk mixture is lukewarm stir in the dissolved yeast. Then stir in 3 1/2 cups flour. When mixed thoroughly cover the bowl with a thick towel and set in a warm place to rise. When the mixture is light (has risen) work in enough flour to make a soft, pliable dough. Knead it well to assure all ingredients are thoroughly blended. Cover again with the towel and set aside to rise. It should rise to about double in size. Then turn the dough out on a floured board (or coun-tertop). Roll it out into a 3/4-inch-thick sheet. Take a sharp knife and cut the dough into pieces 2 1/2 inches long by 1 inch wide. Place these strips close together in a shal-low buttered baking pan. Cover again with the towel and let them rise until light. Then take the towel off and place the pan in a quick oven (400 to 425 degrees). Bake for 15 minutes.

COLONIAL ERA TEA ROLLS

1 cup milk, scalded	1/4 cup sugar
1 cake yeast	1 teaspoon salt

3 1/2 cups flour   Pinch of nutmeg
1/4 cup butter, melted   2 eggs, well beaten

Put the scalding hot milk into a large wooden mixing bowl. Crumble the yeast in 1/4 cup warm water and let it dissolve. When the milk is lukewarm add 2 cups of the flour. Beat well and add the yeast mixture to this. Cover the bowl with a thick towel and set it in a warm place to rise. When it is light (has risen) stir in the melted butter, sugar, salt, nutmeg, and the frothy beaten eggs. Lastly add the rest of the flour and mix thoroughly until it forms a smooth soft dough. Turn the dough out on a floured board (or countertop) and knead hard for 15 minutes. Cover again with the towel and set aside to rise. When the dough has risen break it into small egg-sized chunks and form them into small rolls. Place these rolls close together in a shallow buttered baking pan. Cover again and let rise until light. Bake in a quick oven (400 to 425 degrees) for 15 minutes.

THE TOMPKINS FAMILY'S DELICATE RICE BREAD

4 cups water, warm   4 cups flour
3/4 cup yeast[2]   6 cups milk, warm
1 tablespoon sugar   2 1/4 cups rice flour
2 tablespoons butter

Pour the warm water into a large wooden mixing bowl. Beat in the yeast, sugar, butter, and flour. Cover with a heavy towel and set aside in a warm place to rise for 5 hours. Then stir in the warm milk. Wet the rice flour with a little cold milk until it becomes a thin paste. Boil it for 4 minutes. Allow to cool and when about 100 degrees, stir into the previously made batter. If the blend is

2. Recipes in *Natural Baking the Old Fashioned Way*, by the author.

not thick enough to work into a good dough, add a little more flour. Then turn the dough out on a floured board (or countertop). Knead it thoroughly for at least 15 minutes. Form into loaves, cover with the towel, and let rise again until they are light. Then bake in a moderately quick oven (375 degrees). *Note*: This is a nice and delicate bread for invalids. It keeps well. If you cannot procure rice flour, boil 1 cup whole rice to a thin paste. Mash and beat it smooth. Use this in place of the rice flour called for in the recipe. This was the uncontested favorite of all members of the Tompkins family. D. D. Tompkins served as vice-president under James Monroe from 1817 to 1825.

OLD NEW ENGLAND WHOLE WHEAT BISCUITS

1 cup flour	1 cup whole wheat flour
1 teaspoon salt	6 tablespoons butter, soft
3 teaspoons baking powder	1/2 cup milk

Sift the flour, salt, and baking powder together in a large wooden mixing bowl. Stir in the whole wheat flour and blend well. Cream in the soft butter. Lastly add the milk and work the mixture into a soft dough. Turn it out on a lightly floured board (or countertop) and knead for 5 minutes. Then roll the dough out into a 3/4-inch-thick sheet. Cut into 3-inch round biscuits. Place them close together on a shallow buttered baking pan. Bake in a very quick oven (450 degrees) for from 15 to 18 minutes.

GREAT-GRANDMOTHER MITCHELL'S PRIZE PUMPERNICKEL BREAD

1 1/2 cups water, warm	3 tablespoons caraway seeds
	2 3/4 cups rye flour, sifted

3 packs dry yeast	2 tablespoons butter, soft
1/2 cup molasses	3 3/4 cups flour, sifted
3 1/2 teaspoons salt	

Put the warm water into a large wooden mixing bowl. Add the yeast and stir until it dissolves. Blend in the molasses, salt, and caraway seeds. Put in the rye flour and butter. Blend it well with a large wooden spoon. When smooth add the regular flour and thoroughly mix it with the hands. Turn the dough out onto a lightly floured board (or countertop). Knead hard for at least 10 minutes. Cover with a heavy towel and set aside to rise in a warm place. It should double in bulk within 2 hours. Test by pressing your fingers into the dough. Indentations will be left if it has risen enough. Then punch the dough down hard. Cover and let it rise again. It should almost double in size within 40 minutes. When risen cut the dough in half and shape it into 2 round, slightly flattened loaves. Butter a shallow baking sheet and sprinkle it liberally with cornmeal. Place the rye loaves on opposite corners of the pan. Cover with a damp towel and set aside to rise for 1 hour. Then remove the towel and put the loaves into a moderate oven (350 degrees). Bake for about 35 minutes, or until the loaves are nicely browned.

OLD-TIME RUSKS IN THE COLONIES

2 cups milk, warm	1/2 cup butter
1 cake yeast	2 eggs, well beaten
Flour to suit	1 teaspoon salt
1/2 cup sugar	1 cup raisins

Put the warm milk into a large wooden mixing bowl. Crumble the yeast cake and dissolve it in the warm milk. Then add sufficient flour to make a thick batter. Cover the bowl with a heavy towel and set aside in a warm place to rise. Beat the sugar and butter to a cream in another bowl. Blend in the frothy beaten eggs. Add this to the *risen* batter in the first bowl. Also stir in the salt, raisins, and enough flour to form a soft, pliable dough. Break the dough into chunks about the size of a large egg. Mold with your hands into smooth balls. Set these close together in a shallow buttered baking pan. Cover again and let them rise to double in size. Then uncover and brush the tops with beaten egg white. Sprinkle with cinnamon and sugar. Bake in a quick oven (400 to 425 degrees) for 30 minutes. *Note*: Nuts were often substituted for raisins in the early days.

EARLY SOUTHERN PLANTATION POPOVER MUFFINS

2 cups flour
1 teaspoon butter
2 cups milk

2 eggs, well beaten
1 teaspoon salt

Put the flour into a large wooden mixing bowl. Rub in the butter. Then add the milk, frothy beaten eggs, and salt. Stir well until everything is thoroughly blended. When ready put the mixture into individual buttered cups or a muffin tin. Fill each cup about 2/3 full. Bake in a quick oven (400 to 425 degrees) for 15 minutes. Serve while hot with a sweet sauce.[3]

SCOTT'S FAVORITE MEXICAN CORN BREAD DELUXE

1 1/4 cups cornmeal
1/2 teaspoon baking soda

1 cup milk
3 cups cheese, shredded

---

3. Recipes in Chapter 4.

3/4 teaspoon salt   1 onion, grated
3 cups creamed corn[4]   2 red peppers,
2 eggs, well beaten   chopped fine
1/4 cup butter, melted

Blend the cornmeal, baking soda, and salt in a large wooden mixing bowl. Stir in the creamed corn, frothy beaten eggs, melted butter, milk, and 1 cup of the cheese. When thoroughly blended pour 1/2 the batter into a well-buttered 10-inch-square baking pan. Then blend the rest of the cheese, onion, and red peppers together. Sprinkle this over the batter in the pan. Pour the remaining batter over this. Bake in a moderate oven (350 degrees) for 45 minutes, or until done. Serve while hot. *Note*: General Winfield Scott (1786–1866) became acquainted with this delicious cornmeal dish when he served during the Mexican War in 1847. He won the now-forgotten battles of Cerro Gordo, Contreras, and Churubusco. This man was nominated as Whig candidate for the presidency, but was unsuccessful.

VIENNA ROLLS IN EARLY PENNSYLVANIA

4 cups water, warm   1 cake yeast, crumbled
2 tablespoons sugar   Flour to suit
1 tablespoon salt

Put the warm water into a large wooden mixing bowl. Blend in the sugar, salt, and yeast. When the yeast is dissolved work in enough sifted flour to make a medium soft dough. Knead it well to assure all ingredients are well blended. Cover the bowl with a thick towel and set aside in a warm place to rise. When light (risen) turn the dough out on a floured board (or countertop). Break into large chunks

---

4. Recipe in *Natural Cooking the Old Fashioned Way*, by the author.

and shape into small, tapered loaves, about 6 inches long and 2 inches around. Place these loaves on a shallow buttered baking pan. Allow a little space between the loaves. Cover again and set aside to rise. When light, gash the tops diagonally 3 times. Bake in a moderate oven (350 degrees) for about 25 minutes. *Note*: For a delightful change do not gash the rolls. Try them brushed with beaten egg and sprinkled with poppy seeds.

GREAT-GREAT-GRANDMOTHER HORTON'S ROLLED OATS MUFFINS

1 cup milk, scalded	2 tablespoons butter, melted
2/3 cup rolled oats	1 1/2 cups flour
3 tablespoons maple syrup	4 teaspoons baking powder
1/2 teaspoon salt	1 egg, well beaten

Put the scalded milk and rolled oats into a large wooden mixing bowl and let it stand for 10 minutes. Then stir in the maple syrup, salt, and melted butter. Beat thoroughly. Sift the flour and baking powder together. Stir this into the mixture in the bowl. Beat in the frothy egg. Pour the batter into a well-buttered muffin tin. Fill each cup about 2/3 full. Bake in a hot oven (400 to 425 degrees) for 20 to 30 minutes.

12

Creative Coffeecakes with Natural Foods

GREAT-GRANDMOTHER MITCHELL'S
SESAME PASTRY TREAT

5 tablespoons olive oil
2 tablespoons sugar
1/4 teaspoon salt
1 tablespoon lemon juice

1 cup flour
1/4 teaspoon baking
  powder

Put 1/4 cup cold water into a large wooden mixing bowl. Beat in the olive oil, sugar, salt, and lemon juice. Sift the flour and baking powder together. Now blend these with the ingredients in the bowl. Work the mixture well until it forms a smooth, pliable dough. Turn the dough out on a lightly floured board (or countertop). Roll it out into a 1/8-inch-thick sheet. Cut neatly into 2-inch squares. Then prepare the filling as follows:

1/4 cup almonds,
  chopped fine
1/4 cup sesame seeds

1/4 cup coconut, toasted
1/4 cup honey
3 drops almond extract

Blend all of the above ingredients in a wooden mixing bowl. Put a small ball of the mixture in the center of each pastry square. Fold these squares over the filling. Have the 4 corners overlap in the center to form a triangle. Press firmly together to close. Brush each with beaten egg and sprinkle lightly with sesame seeds. Place them in a shallow buttered baking pan. Bake in a very slow oven (275 to 300 degrees) for about 20 minutes, or until golden brown. When done remove from the oven and sprinkle with powdered sugar. Serve hot or cold. *Note*: This recipe makes about 36 small pastries. It was one of Mrs. Mitchell's very best concoctions.

EARLY AMERICAN FILLED COFFEECAKE SUPREME

3 cups flour	1/2 teaspoon cinnamon
3 teaspoons baking powder	1/2 teaspoon nutmeg
	1/4 cup butter, soft
3/4 cup sugar	3 eggs
1 teaspoon salt	1 cup milk

Blend the flour, baking powder, sugar, salt, and spices. Then sift these ingredients into a large wooden mixing bowl. Beat in the butter. Then stir in the unbeaten eggs and milk. Continue stirring until the dough is lump free and smooth. Put this mixture into a well-buttered round baking pan. Set aside and prepare the topping as follows:

3/4 cup brown sugar	1/4 teaspoon salt
1/4 cup butter, soft	1 teaspoon cinnamon
3 tablespoons flour	1 cup walnuts, chopped fine

Put the brown sugar, butter, flour, salt, and cinnamon

into a wooden mixing bowl and beat to a light, creamy mixture. Spread this over the top of the dough in the pan. Sprinkle with the chopped nuts. Bake in a moderately hot oven (375 degrees) for 25 minutes. When the coffeecake is done take it from the oven and set the pan on a wire rack to cool. Leave it for 10 minutes. Then remove the cake from the pan and set it aside to cool completely. When cold split the cake into 2 layers. Take 1 cup cream and whip it until stiff. Spread this between the layers. Cut as you would a pie and serve.

BEST CIVIL WAR PERIOD COFFEECAKE

1/2 cake yeast	2 cups flour
1 cup milk, scalded	1/4 cup butter, soft
and cooled	1/2 cup sugar
1 tablespoon sugar	1 egg, well beaten
1/2 teaspoon salt	

Crumble the yeast in 1/4 cup lukewarm water and let it dissolve. Meanwhile put the milk into a large wooden bowl. Add the sugar, salt, and flour. Stir well and blend in the yeast. Cover the bowl with a thick towel and set it in a warm place to rise overnight. In the morning blend in the soft butter, sugar, and egg. Work in enough flour to make a very soft and pliable dough. Break the dough into 2 equal pieces. Place each in a buttered shallow pan. Cover again and let rise until very light. Then uncover and rub the cake tops with sugar dissolved in milk. Sprinkle with dry sugar and cinnamon. Bake in a moderate oven (350 degrees) for about 25 minutes. The coffee cake should be about 1 1/2 inches thick when finished. Serve while either warm or cold.

MRS. McCLELLAN'S ROLLED OAT COFFEE CAKE

1 cup rolled oats	1 teaspoon baking soda
1 1/4 cups water, boiling	1/2 teaspoon salt
2 eggs	1 teaspoon cinnamon
1/2 cup butter, soft	1/4 teaspoon nutmeg
1 cup sugar	1/4 cup walnuts,
1 cup brown sugar	chopped
1 1/3 cups flour	

Put the rolled oats into a large wooden mixing bowl and pour the boiling water over them. Let it stand for 20 minutes. Then beat in the eggs, butter, and sugar. In a separate bowl blend the flour, baking soda, salt, spices, and nuts. Stir these ingredients into those in the first bowl. Blend everything well and put into a large, well-buttered shallow baking pan. Lightly rub the top of the coffeecake with melted butter. Sprinkle with cinnamon and finely chopped nutmeats. Bake in a moderate oven (350 degrees) for 35 to 45 minutes. When done sprinkle it with powdered sugar. Serve while hot or cold. *Note*: George Brinton McClellan's (1826–85) mother made him this coffeecake as a boy. He went on to become the Union general who defeated Lee at Antietam, Maryland, on September 16, 1862. McClellan was unsuccessful in his bid for the presidency in 1864.

OLD NEW ENGLAND APPLE COFFEECAKE

1/2 cup milk	2 tablespoons baking powder
1/4 cup butter, melted	1/2 teaspoon salt
2 eggs, well beaten	1 teaspoon cinnamon
1 1/2 cups flour	2 cups apples, chopped
1/2 cup sugar	

Blend the milk, butter, and frothy beaten eggs in a large wooden mixing bowl. Sift together the flour, sugar, baking powder, salt, and cinnamon. Repeat this 3 times. Then add these dry ingredients to those in the mixing bowl. Beat very hard. Lastly blend in the apples. Pour the batter into a well-buttered square baking pan. Set aside while the following is prepared:

1 tablespoon butter, soft	2 tablespoons flour
1/4 cup sugar	1 teaspoon cinnamon
1 teaspoon nuts, finely chopped	Pinch of nutmeg

Blend all of the above ingredients in a small wooden mixing bowl. Work them together until you have a good, crumbly mixture. Sprinkle this over the batter in the pan. Put into a quick oven (400 degrees) and bake for 30 minutes. When the cake is done take it from the oven and set it on a wire rack to cool. Leave for 10 minutes. Then take the cake from the pan and put it on a large dish to finish cooling. Serve while either warm or cold.

GREAT-GREAT-GRANDMOTHER HORTON'S BREAKFAST JELLY ROLL

1/3 cup water, hot	1 cup sugar
2 eggs	1 1/2 teaspoons baking powder
1 tablespoon butter, melted	1/4 teaspoon salt
1 teaspoon lemon extract	
1 cup flour, sifted	

Blend the hot water, eggs, melted butter, and lemon extract in a large wooden mixing bowl. Sift together the flour, sugar, baking powder, and salt. Then add these dry ingredients to those in the bowl. Beat very hard until the mixture is smooth. Pour the batter into a large, well-buttered and thickly floured, shallow baking pan. The batter should be about 1/2 inch thick or less. Bake in a moderate oven (350 degrees) for 20 minutes. The cake should be done but not brown in order to roll it successfully Use a wide spatula and work the cake gently out of the pan. While still warm, turn the cake out on a towel wrung out in hot water. Cut off any crisp edges. Spread the cake thickly with a soft, tart jelly or jam.[1] Roll it up lightly and quickly before it cools. Wrap with the wet towel. Allow the cake to remain in the towel for 20 to 30 minutes so that it will hold together. Then remove the towel and sprinkle the cake with powdered sugar.

ORIGINAL OLD-TIME
CRANBERRY-APPLE COFFEECAKE

1/2 cup butter	1 teaspoon cinnamon
1 cup sugar	1/2 teaspoon mace
1 egg	1/2 teaspoon nutmeg
2 cups flour, sifted	1/3 cup orange juice
2 teaspoons baking powder	1 1/2 tablespoons orange rind, grated
1/2 teaspoon baking soda	1 cup fresh cranberries, chopped
1/2 teaspoon salt	1 cup apples, grated

Cream the butter and sugar in a large wooden mixing bowl. When it is light and fluffy add the egg and beat thoroughly. In a separate bowl combine the flour, baking powder, baking soda, salt, and spices. Sift these ingredients into the mixture

---

1. Recipes in *Natural Cooking the Old Fashioned Way*, by the author.

in the first bowl, alternately with the orange juice. Lastly blend in the orange rind, cranberries, and apples. Pour the batter into a well-buttered and lightly floured shallow baking pan. Bake in a moderate oven (350 degrees) for 1 1/4 hours, or until the edges shrink away from the sides of the pan. When done, the center of the coffeecake should spring back to the touch. Let it cool for 10 minutes before taking from the pan.

GREAT-GRANDMOTHER SHAW'S PUMPKIN COFFEECAKE

1/2 cup olive oil	1/4 teaspoon salt
2 eggs	1 teaspoon baking soda
1/3 cup water, warm	1/2 teaspoon nutmeg
1 cup pumpkin, mashed	1 teaspoon cinnamon
1 2/3 cups flour, sifted	1 cup nuts, chopped
1 1/4 cups sugar	1/2 cup cherries, chopped

Blend the olive oil, eggs, water, and pumpkin in a large wooden mixing bowl. Beat hard together. Then sift together the flour, sugar, salt, baking soda, and spices. Gradually add these dry ingredients to those in the mixing bowl. Beat hard until it is smooth and creamy. Lastly stir in the nuts and cherries. Pour the batter into a well-buttered and floured shallow baking pan. Sprinkle the top with finely chopped nutmeats. Bake in a moderate oven (350 degrees) for 1 hour. When done take the coffee cake from the oven and sprinkle over the top with powedered sugar. Serve while hot or when cold.

PRIZE CINNAMON ROLLS IN THE COLONIES

1 1/4 cups milk, hot	Flour to suit
3 eggs, well beaten	1/2 cup butter, melted

Sugar to suit
1 teaspoon salt
2 cakes yeast

Butter to suit, soft
Cinnamon to suit
Nuts to suit, chopped

Put the scalding hot milk into a large wooden mixing bowl and set aside until it becomes lukewarm. Beat in the frothy beaten egg whites, 1/2 cup sugar, and the salt. Crumble the yeast and dissolve it in a little warm water. Stir this into the mixture. Add 3 cups flour and the melted butter. Blend well and then work in enough flour to make a soft, pliable dough. Put this dough into a large buttered bowl and cover with a heavy towel. Set aside in a warm place to rise until it has doubled in size. Then turn the dough out on a lightly floured board (or countertop). Roll it out into a 1/2-inch-thick sheet. Spread the sheet with soft butter. Sprinkle generously with cinnamon sugar, and nuts. Carefully roll the sheet up like a scroll and cut into 1/2 inch slices. Lay each slice in a well-buttered shallow baking pan. Baste with more melted butter and sprinkle the tops with cinnamon, sugar, and finely chopped nuts. Set aside to rise again. When double in size bake in a moderate oven (350 degrees) for about 25 minutes. The rolls should be nicely browned.

MUHLENBERG'S DRIED APPLE COFFEECAKE

1 cup dried apples,
    chopped fine
1 cup molasses
    or
1 cup honey
1 cup sugar
1/2 cup butter, soft
2 eggs

1/2 cup sour milk
    or
1/2 cup coffee, strong
1 teaspoon baking soda
1 teaspoon cloves
1 teaspoon cinnamon
1 teaspoon allspice
Flour to suit

Put the dried apples into a saucepan with a little water and let them stew for 10 minutes. Then add the molasses or honey and simmer for 1 full hour. When done set aside to cool. Meanwhile take a large wooden mixing bowl and cream the sugar, and butter. Beat in the eggs, sour milk or coffee, baking soda, and spices. When the apple mixture has cooled to lukewarm stir it in with these ingredients. Lastly work in enough flour to make a stiff batter. Pour it into a well-buttered and floured shallow baking pan. Bake in a moderately quick oven (375 degrees) until done. *Note*: This is an old German recipe concocted by the Muhlenberg family many years ago. John (1746–1807) was a general during the Revolutionary War. He was commander-in-chief in Virginia until the arrival of Steuben. This man was in Congress between 1789 and 1801.

13

Electrifying Old-time
Natural Cakes and Cookies

MRS. HOOKER'S OLD-FASHIONED 3-LAYER CAKE

1 1/2 cups sugar
1 cup butter, soft
3 eggs
1 1/4 cups raspberry jam
3 cups flour, sifted
1/2 teaspoon baking soda

1 teaspoon baking powder
1/2 teaspoon salt
1/2 teaspoon cloves
1 teaspoon cinnamon
1/2 teaspoon nutmeg
1 cup buttermilk

Put the sugar and butter in a large wooden mixing bowl and beat them to a light creamy mixture. Add the eggs, one at a time, and beat thoroughly. Lastly beat in the raspberry jam. Now sift together the flour, baking soda, baking powder, salt, and spices. Then add these dry ingredients in 3 parts, alternately with the buttermilk. Beat thoroughly after each part is put in.

Butter 3 round 9-inch cake pans and line them with buttered and lightly floured paper. Pour equal amounts of the batter into each of the 3 pans. Bake in a moderate oven (350 degrees) for 30 to 40 minutes, or until a toothpick inserted in the center comes out clean. Then take out of the oven and set the pans on wire racks to cool for 10 minutes. Then turn the cakes out of the pans and set aside until cold. When completely cold spread each layer with old fashioned boiled white frosting.[1] Set 1 layer on the other and cover the entire cake with the same. *Note*: This old-time layer cake gained some degree of fame as a specialty of General Hooker's mother, long before the Civil War. This man was the Union general who was defeated by General Lee at Chancellorsville in May of 1863. He later defeated Bragg at the battle of Lookout Mountain on November 24 of that same year.

EARLY BOSTONIAN RAISIN COOKIES

1 cup butter	Pinch of salt
1 1/2 cups sugar	1 1/2 cups raisins,
3 egg whites, stiffly	chopped fine
beaten	1/2 nutmeg, grated
3 egg yolks, well beaten	Flour to suit
1/2 teaspoon baking soda	

Cream the butter and sugar in a large wooden mixing bowl. Stir in the fluffy beaten egg whites. Then stir in the custardlike beaten egg yolks. Blend in the baking soda, salt, raisins, and nutmeg. Lastly add enough flour to make a very stiff batter. This should not be thick enough to roll out or mold. Spread in spoonfuls on a baking pan lined with buttered paper. Bake in a quick oven (400 to 425 degrees) until lightly browned.

---

1. Recipe in *Natural Baking the Old Fashioned Way*, by the author.

GREAT-GREAT-GRANDMOTHER HORTON'S SILVER CAKE

2 cups sugar
1 cup butter
3 cups flour
3 teaspoons baking powder

1 cup milk
1 teaspoon almond extract
8 egg whites, stiffly beaten

Put the sugar and butter into a large wooden mixing bowl and beat to a light creamy mixture. Then sift together the flour and baking powder 3 times. Alternately beat this and the milk into the bowl. Blend in the almond extract. Lastly fold in the fluffy beaten egg whites. Pour the batter into a well-buttered tube pan. Bake in a moderate oven (325 to 350 degrees) for about 50 minutes. When the cake is done, start preparing the following icing:

2 cups powdered sugar
4 tablespoons cream

1/2 teaspoon vanilla
1 cup coconut, grated

Put the sugar into a wooden mixing bowl. Gradually add the cream and beat steadily. Add the vanilla. When beaten to a good spreading consistency, spread all over the cake. Sprinkle heavily with the grated coconut.

OLD-FASHIONED ENGLISH COCONUT COOKIES

1 cup milk
1/2 teaspoon baking soda
2/3 cup butter, melted
2 cups sugar

1 cup coconut, grated
1 teaspoon cream of tartar
Flour to suit

Put the milk into a large wooden mixing bowl. Dissolve the baking soda in the milk. Stir in the melted butter, sugar, and coconut. Sift the cream of tartar with a little flour. Beat this into the mixture. Then add sufficient flour to make a soft dough. Put the dough on a floured board (or countertop) and roll it out in a 1/4-inch-thick sheet. Cut into small round cookies. Place them on a buttered shallow baking tin. Bake in a quick oven (400 to 425 degrees) until lightly browned.

GREAT-GRANDMOTHER SHAW'S PEANUT BUTTER COOKIES

1/2 cup butter	1 1/4 cups flour
1/2 cup peanut butter	3/4 teaspoon baking soda
1/2 cup sugar	1/4 teaspoon salt
1/2 cup brown sugar	1/2 teaspoon baking
1 egg	powder

Beat all of the above ingredients together in a large wooden mixing bowl. When well blended set it on ice to chill. Break off small balls of the mixture and lay them on a lightly buttered baking pan. Leave about 3 inches between them. Then press each ball down with the prongs of a fork. Bake in a moderate oven (350 degrees) for 10 to 12 minutes.

MRS. BOONE'S OLD-TIME HERMIT COOKIES

1 cup butter	1/2 teaspoon cloves
1 1/2 cups sugar	1/2 teaspoon allspice
3 eggs, well beaten	1 teaspoon cinnamon
1 cup raisins, chopped	Flour to suit

Beat all of the above ingredients together in a large wooden mixing bowl. Blend in enough flour to make a moderately stiff dough. Put the dough on a floured board (or countertop) and roll it out in a 1/4-inch-thick sheet. Cut into small square cookies. Place them on a buttered shallow baking pan. Bake in a moderate oven (350 degrees). *Note*: If the bottom of a pan, turned upside down is used, the cookies can be removed much more easily. This old cookie recipe originated in the family of Daniel Boone (1735–1820), the pioneer who is noted for his many daring exploits against the Indians. Boone's remains are interred near Frankfort, Kentucky.

CIVIL WAR APPLESAUCE-FRUIT-NUT CAKE

1 1/2 cups rolled oats	1 cup candied cherries
1 cup applesauce	1 cup walnuts, chopped
1/4 cup molasses	2 1/2 cups flour, sifted
or	1 teaspoon baking soda
1/4 cup honey	1 teaspoon salt
1 cup brown sugar	1 teaspoon cinnamon
1 cup raisins	3/4 teaspoon cloves
1 cup candied fruit	1/2 teaspoon nutmeg

Put the rolled oats into a large wooden mixing bowl. Stir in the applesauce, molasses or honey, and the brown sugar. In another bowl blend the fruits, nuts, and 1/2 cup flour. Sift the remaining 2 cups flour with the baking soda, salt, and the spices. Then combine all of these ingredients in the wooden mixing bowl and stir until thoroughly blended. Pour the batter into 2 well-buttered loaf pans which have been lined with buttered paper. Bake in a slow oven (300 to 325 degrees) for 1 hour. Test the cakes by piercing them with a toothpick. If it comes out clean the cakes are done. Take out of the oven and set them on wire racks to cool for 10 minutes. Then remove the cakes from the pans. Set aside for 2 or 3 days before serving. This type of old-fashioned cake will stay moist and fresh-tasting for a long time.

GREAT-GRANDMOTHER MITCHELL'S HOMEMADE VANILLA WAFERS

2/3 cup butter	1 teaspoon cream of
1 cup sugar	tartar
1 egg, well beaten	Flour to suit
1/2 teaspoon baking soda	1 tablespoon vanilla
4 tablespoons milk	

Cream the butter and sugar in a large wooden mixing bowl. Stir in the frothy beaten egg. Dissolve the baking soda in the milk and add this next. Sift the cream of tartar with 1 cup flour. Then blend this in with the rest of the ingredients. Lastly stir in the vanilla. After thoroughly beating the mixture, blend in enough flour to make a rather soft dough. It must be able to be rolled without sticking. Put the dough on a floured board (or countertop) and roll it out in a 1/4-inch-thick sheet. Cut into small round cookies. Turn a wide baking pan upside down. Butter it and place the cookies upon it. Bake in a quick oven (400 to 425 degrees).

GREAT-GRANDMOTHER MITCHELL'S FAIRY GINGER COOKIES

Make these exactly as described for the above vanilla wafers, except substitute 1 tablespoon ginger for the vanilla called for in the recipe.

OLD PLANTATION ROLLED OAT BANANA CAKE

1 cup sugar	1 1/2 teaspoons baking
1/2 cup butter	soda
1 teaspoon vanilla	1/2 teaspoon salt
2 eggs, well beaten	1/2 cup buttermilk
1 1/4 cups flour, sifted	1 1/4 cups rolled oats
1/2 teaspoon baking powder	1 1/4 cups banana,
	mashed

Put the sugar, butter, and vanilla into a large wooden mixing bowl. Beat until you have a light creamy mixture. Whip in the frothy beaten eggs, one at a time. Then sift together the flour, baking powder, baking soda, and salt. Add these to the bowl, alternately with the buttermilk. Beat hard after each part is put in. Then stir in the rolled oats and lastly the bananas. Pour the batter into 2 round 9-inch, well-buttered and floured cake pans. Bake in a moderate oven (350 degrees) for 25 to 30 minutes. Test the cake by inserting a toothpick in the center. If it comes out clean the cake is done. When finished baking take the cakes from the oven and set them on wire racks to cool for 10 minutes. Then turn out the cakes and set aside until cold. When they are cold spread each layer with homemade chocolate frosting.[2] Set one layer upon the other and cover with the same frosting.

---

2. Recipe in *Natural Baking the Old Fashioned Way*, by the author.

14

Delectable Desserts with Natural Foods

THE SCHUYLER FAMILY'S FAMOUS TEA ROLL

Note: This is a very old recipe which dates back to Colonial times and the family of General John Philip Schuyler (1733-1804). He served as a Captain in the English army during the French and Indian War in 1756. This famous man was a member of the colonial assembly in 1768 and a delegate to the Continental Congress in 1775.

1 cup flour
1 teaspoon baking powder
1 teaspoon ginger
1 teaspoon cinnamon
1/2 teaspoon salt
1 cup sugar
4 eggs, well beaten
1 tablespoon lemon juice
1 tablespoon lemon rind, grated
1 tablespoon orange juice
1 tablespoon orange rind, grated
1/2 cup tea, extremely strong
Powdered sugar to suit
2 cups fresh peaches, diced
3 cups cream, whipped

Sift together the flour, baking powder, spices, and salt. Set aside while you gradually whip the sugar into the frothy beaten eggs. Blend in the lemon juice and rind, orange juice and rind, and the tea. Lastly stir in the sifted flour mixture. Beat hard and then pour this batter into a large, shallow, well-buttered and floured baking pan. Bake in a quick oven (400 degrees) for about 15 minutes. While the cake is baking sprinkle a large towel with powdered sugar. When the cake is done turn it out of the pan, onto the towel, while it is still hot. Roll it up in the towel and place this on a wire rack to cool for 1 hour. When the cake is cold take the fresh peaches and blend them with the stiffly whipped cream. Unroll the cake and thickly spread it with the peach-cream mixture. Roll it back up and lay it on a platter with the seam facing down. Spread the remaining peach-cream blend all over the outside of the cake. Set it on ice for 1 hour. This cake should be thoroughly chilled before serving. Garnish it with slices of fresh peaches.

GREAT-GREAT-GRANDMOTHER HORTON'S BEST PIE CRUST

4 cups flour	1 1/2 cups butter
3 teaspoons baking powder	Ice water to suit

Sift the flour and baking powder together twice. Then put it into a large wooden mixing bowl. With a broad-bladed knife chop 3/4 cup of the butter into the flour until it looks like yellow sand. Gradually work in some ice water until you have a stiff dough. Do this with a large wooden spoon until it is no longer possible to move the spoon. Then make the dough into a ball with your floured hands. Handle as little as possible. Lay the dough on a floured board or countertop) and roll it out into a very thin sheet. Always roll away from you with a light quick action. When thin enough baste with 1/3 the remaining butter. In other words, stick tiny pieces of butter in regular close rows all over the sheet of dough. Use a knife for this purpose rather than your hands. Sprinkle a little flour lightly over the sheet. Then tightly roll up the dough into close folds. Flatten it enough so the rolling pin can take hold and proceed to roll the dough out into a thin sheet a second time. Baste again with another 1/3 of the butter and sprinkle lightly with flour as you did before. Roll the sheet of dough up again, flatten, and roll it out again in a sheet. Baste a last time with the remaining butter and again sprinkle with flour. And roll the dough up again. Before you roll out the dough the final time, you should chill it for at least 15 minutes, and as much as 1 hour if time permits. The finished pie crust will turn out to be flakier and firmer. After properly cooling the dough, roll it out into your crust. Butter the pie pans. Lay the sheet of dough in each pan. Cut evenly around the edge of each pan after neatly fitting the dough sheet into it. All cutting scraps may be reused by simply piling them together and rolling them out again into a thin sheet. The top crust (if one is used) is made by laying the dough across the pie and cutting it to fit (after the pan has beeen filled). The edges are then pressed down with a knife edge or a spoon.

FRESH PEACH PIE ON THE OLD PLANTATION

Peel, stone, and slice some fresh peaches. Line a pie plate with a good crust. Lay in the peach slices and sprinkle sugar liberally over them in proportion to their natural sweetness. Very ripe peaches require comparatively little sugar. Chop 3 peach kernels up fine for each pie being made. Sprinkle this on the peaches. Pour in a very little water. Use an upper crust or cross-bars of crust, over the top. Bake in a hot oven (400 degrees) for 50 minutes. Sift powdered sugar over the top after the pie has finished baking.

or

Some old-timers preferred to pare the peaches and put whole into the unbaked pie shell. The peaches must be tightly packed together, and freely sweetened. In this case they should be covered entirely with an upper crust and then baked as above.

CHRISTMAS DATE PUDDING
IN EARLY NEW ENGLAND

1 cup dates, chopped fine	1 cup flour
1 cup water, boiling	3/4 cup pecans, chopped
1 teaspoon baking soda	1 teaspoon baking
1 cup sugar	powder
1/4 cup butter	1/2 teaspoon salt
1 egg, well beaten	1/2 teaspoon cinnamon
1 teaspoon vanilla	

Blend the dates, boiling water, and baking soda in a large wooden mixing bowl. Set aside to cool. Meanwhile cream the sugar and butter in another bowl. Beat in the rest of the ingredients in the sequence given above. Add this mixture to that in the first bowl. Stir thoroughly together and pour it into a buttered baking dish. Bake in a moderate oven (350 degrees) for 30 to 40 minutes. When the pudding is done, the following sauce topping should be prepared:

1 1/4 cups dates, diced	3/4 cup water
1/2 cup sugar	1 tablespoon flour,
3/4 cup pecans, halved	heaping

Blend all of the above ingredients in a saucepan. Bring to a boil and then let it simmer for 5 minutes, or until it thickens nicely. Stir continuously. Spread this sauce over the top of the baked pudding. Return the pudding to the oven and leave it for 5 minutes. Then take it out and set aside to cool. *Note*: This old fashioned pudding is always better when made the night before and served with the Christmas dinner the next day.

MRS. BUTLER'S FAMOUS BREAD PUDDING

4 cups bread crumbs, soft	3 eggs, well beaten
	1/2 teaspoon salt
2 cups milk	1 teaspoon cinnamon
4 tablespoons butter	1/2 teaspoon nutmeg
1/2 cup sugar	1 cup raisins

Place the bread crumbs in a buttered baking dish. Place the milk and butter in a saucepan and heat to scalding. Meanwhile blend the sugar, frothy beaten eggs, spices, and raisins. Stir a little of the hot milk-butter mixture into this. Then gradually stir the entire milk-butter mixture in. Blend thoroughly and then pour it over the bread crumbs in the baking dish. Bake in a moderate oven (350 degrees) for 45 minutes. Test by inserting a silver knife 1 inch from the edge of the pudding. If it comes out clean the pudding is done. *Note*: This very old recipe has been in the Butler family for untold years. Mrs. Butler used to make it for her son who later gained fame as a noted Union general. He teamed up with Admiral Farragut and won an important Civil War victory in the battle of New Orleans on April 24, 1862.

OLD-FASHIONED CHERRY PIE IN VIRGINIA

Line a pie tin with a good crust.[1] Fill it with fresh, ripe pitted cherries. Sprinkle sugar over them in proportion to their natural sweetness. Cover with a top crust, pinch down the edges, and bake in a hot oven (400 degrees) for about 45 minutes. Eat when cold, with powdered sugar sprinkled all over the top. *Note*: Blackberry, plum, raspberry, and ripe gooseberry pies are all made in exactly the same way.

WONDERFUL OLDEN-DAY CRANBERRY TARTS

Wash and pick over the fresh cranberries. Put them into a porcelain kettle with just enough water to prevent burning. Simmer until they burst open and become soft. Then run the cranberries through a colander to remove the skins. Sweeten to taste. Pour into small unbaked pastry tart shells.[2] Cross strips of pastry over the top. Bake in a hot oven (400 degrees) for about 40 minutes.

GREAT-GREAT-GRANDMOTHER HORTON'S FRESH COCONUT PUDDING

2 tablespoons gelatin	1 coconut, grated
2 cups cream	1 teaspoon almond extract
2 cups sugar	3 cups cream, whipped

Soak the gelatin in 1/2 cup cold water until it dissolves. Put the 2 cups cream into a saucepan and let it come to a boil. Stir in the sugar, dissolved gelatin, 2 cups grated coco-

---

1. Recipe included herein.
2. Recipe included herein.

nut, and the almond extract. Beat together thoroughly. Then pour it into a bowl and put on ice until it begins to "set." When chilled carefully fold in the stiffly whipped cream. Spoon the mixture into a large ring mold or a pudding dish. Sprinkle the rest of the grated coconut over the top. Set aside in a cool place until the following day. Serve with a side dish of homemade butterscotch sauce.[3]

CURRANT-RASPBERRY TARTS
BEFORE THE CIVIL WAR

To every 3 cups fresh currants allow 1 cup raspberries. Blend them together well and sweeten abundantly. Then put them into small unbaked pastry tart shells.[4] Cover with a top crust and bake in a hot oven (400 degrees) for about 40 minutes. Eat when cold with sugar sifted over the top.

ALEXANDER H. STEPHENS'S
FAVORITE CREAMY RICE PUDDING

more use eggs like custard

4 cups milk	1 cup cream
1/4 teaspoon salt	2 eggs, well beaten
1/2 cup rice, long	1/2 cup sugar
grained	1 teaspoon vanilla
1/2 cup raisins	Nutmeg to suit

Put the milk and salt into a saucepan. When warm, add the rice and bring to a quick boil. Then let it simmer for 15 minutes. Stir occasionally. Add the raisins and let it all simmer together for 5 minutes longer. Stir in 1/4 cup of the cream and simmer for 3 more minutes. Meanwhile, in a

---

3. Recipe in Chapter 4.
4. Recipe included herein.

wooden mixing bowl, combine the frothy beaten eggs, sugar, vanilla, and the rest of the cream. Blend well and stir in a little of the hot rice mixture from the sauce-pan. Then dump the contents of the mixing bowl into the saucepan and simmer slowly until it begins to thicken. At this point, pour the pudding into a bowl and stir often un-til it cools completely. Serve cold with nutmeg sprinkled over the top. *Note*: Alexander H. Stephens is an often forgotten man in the history of our great country. And who was he, you ask? Stephens was vice-president of the Confederacy under Jefferson Davis in 1861.

ORIGINAL OLD-TIME STRAWBERRY PIE

Wash and carefully pick over some fresh strawberries. Line your pie pan with a good crust.[5] Put in a layer of straw-berries. Sprinkle with a good coating of sugar. Cover with another layer of strawberries. Again liberally sprinkle with sugar. Pack the entire pie shell *very full* in this sequence, because strawberries tend to shrink a lot during baking. Cover with a top crust, pinch down the edges, and immedi-ately bake in a hot oven (400 degrees) for about 40 min-utes. *Note*: The real old-fashioned huckleberry pie is made in exactly the same way.

GREAT-GRANDMOTHER MITCHELL'S
CHRISTMAS CRANBERRY PUDDING

3/4 cup butter	1/2 teaspoon salt
3/4 cup sugar	1/2 cup milk
3 eggs, well beaten	2 cups fresh cranberries,

---

5. Recipe included herein.

2 1/2 cups flour, sifted
2 teaspoons baking
  powder

chopped
3/4 cup walnuts, chopped

Cream the butter and sugar in a large wooden mixing bowl. Then blend in the frothy beaten eggs and whip the mixture very hard. Sift together the flour, baking powder, and salt. Add this, alternately with the milk, to the mixture in the bowl. Beat hard after each addition. Lastly stir in the cranberries and walnuts. Blend well and then pour the pudding batter into a well-buttered and floured baking dish or mold. Cover tightly and place it on the rack in a large kettle. Add enough boiling water to cover 1/2 the dish. Bring to a boil and then gently simmer for 2 full hours. Add more boiling water to the kettle, as needed, to keep the proper liquid level. Then take the cover off the pudding dish. Test the pudding by inserting a silver knife in the center. If it comes out clean the pudding is done. Take the dish or mold from the kettle. Set aside to cool for 15 minutes. Then turn it out on a dish and serve while still warm with a nice sweet sauce.[6]

HOMEMADE COCONUT PIE IN EARLY ALABAMA

3/4 cup butter
1 1/2 cups sugar
1/4 cup white wine
2 tablespoons rosewater

2 1/2 cups coconut,
  grated
1 teaspoon nutmeg
5 egg whites, stiffly
  beaten

Cream the butter and sugar in a large wooden mixing bowl. When well blended, beat very light with the wine and rosewater. Then add the coconut and nutmeg with as little

6. Recipes in Chapter 4.

and as light stirring as possible. Finally fold in the fluffy beaten egg whites with a few skillful strokes. Pour at once into open unbaked pie shells. Bake immediately in a hot oven (400 degrees) for 25 to 30 minutes. Eat the pies when cold with powdered sugar sifted over them. *Note*: These pies are extremely pretty as well as being delightfully tasty.

THE ELLERY FAMILY'S PUMPKIN CUSTARD

1 cup stewed pumpkin, mashed	Pinch of nutmeg
3 eggs, well beaten	1/2 teaspoon cinnamon
3/4 cup brown sugar	2 cups milk, scalding
1/2 teaspoon salt	1 cup cream, whipped

Put the stewed pumpkin into a large wooden mixing bowl. Blend in the frothy beaten eggs, brown sugar, salt, and spices. Stir in the hot milk. Beat the mixture thoroughly and hard. Pour it into a buttered quart baking dish or 6 custard cups. Set in a shallow pan of hot water. Bake in a moderately hot oven (375 degrees) for 25 to 30 minutes, or until firm. Set aside to cool. Serve when cold with whipped cream on top. *Note*: This wonderful old-time pumpkin dish originated with the Ellery family of early Rhode Island. William Ellery (1727–1820) is one of the forgotten signers of the Declaration of Independence.

15

Superb Old-time Natural Breakfast Specials

QUEEN'S TOAST IN THE EARLY SOUTH

Trim the crusts from some slices of stale bread. Fry the slices in boiling butter or oil until they are a fine brown. Quickly dip each slice in boiling water to remove the grease. Sprinkle with powdered sugar, and pile upon a warmed plate. Pour some sweet wine sauce[1] over them while still hot, and serve at once.

MRS. GERRY'S STEWED BREAKFAST POTATOES

6 potatoes, medium sized	Pinch of salt
1 cup milk	Pinch of pepper
2 tablespoons butter, well rounded	1 tablespoon flour

Pare and quarter the potatoes. Put them into a saucepan with just enough salted cold water to cover. Set aside to

1. Recipes in Chapter 4.

soak for 1/2 hour. Then stew them until soft and breaking into pieces. Drain off half the water and replace it with the milk. Boil for 3 minutes while stirring well. Put in the butter, salt, and pepper. Thicken slightly with the flour and bring to a quick boil. Immediately turn the mixture into a covered bowl. *Note*: This is an excellent old-fashioned family dish. Children are usually fond of it, and it is wholesome. Stewed potatoes were a favorite in the Gerry family for a great number of years. Elbridge loved it even in his later years while he was James Madison's vice-president in 1813.

EARLY AMERICAN NOTES ON PANCAKES

Old-timers always used a small frying pan for making their pancakes. They heated the pan and put in a teaspoon or two of lard (we use butter or oil). It was quickly melted and ran all over the bottom of the pan. They then poured in a large ladleful of batter—enough to cover the bottom of the pan with a thin sheet. The pancake was turned with a tin spatula, very carefully, to avoid tearing it. A hot dish was ready and the pancake was turned out upon it. The pancake was covered with powdered sugar. It was rolled dexterously up like a sheet of paper. They were kept hot by setting the dish in the oven until enough were cooked. One-half dozen were sent to the table at once.

GREAT-GREAT-GRANDMOTHER HORTON'S BEST OLD-TIME PANCAKES

6 egg yolks, well beaten	Milk to suit
1/4 teaspoon salt	2 cups flour
Pinch of baking soda, dissolved in vinegar[2]	6 egg whites, stiffly beaten

2. Recipes in *Natural Cooking the Old Fashioned Way*, by the author.

Put the custardlike beaten egg yolks into a large wooden mixing bowl. Stir in the salt, baking soda-vinegar mixture, and 2 cups milk. Then alternately stir in the flour and the fluffy beaten egg whites until both are all used up. Thin with additional milk until the batter is the right consistency. Cook as directed above.

JELLY OR JAM PANCAKES IN THE EARLY 1800S

Mix the batter as directed in the previous recipe. When the pancakes are fried, lay them upon a hot platter. Spread thickly with nice homemade jelly[3] or jam.[4] Roll each pancake neatly up like a scroll. Sprinkle lightly with powdered sugar. Send around the table with wine sauce[5] or sweetened cream.[6]

FABULOUS BUCKWHEAT CAKES
IN EARLY VIRGINIA

1 cake yeast	1 tablespoon salt
9 cups water, warm	1/2 teaspoon baking
Buckwheat flour to suit	soda

At night before retiring dissolve the yeast in 1 cup warm water. Then put this into a large wooden mixing bowl with the remaining warm water. Stir in enough buckwheat flour to make a thick batter. Add the salt and beat the mixture thoroughly. Cover the bowl with a thick towel and set aside in a warm place until morning. The next morning dissolve the baking soda in 1/4 cup warm water. Stir this into the

3. Recipes in *Natural Cooking the Old Fashioned Way*, by the author.
4. Ibid.
5. Recipes in Chapter 4.
6. Recipes in Chapter 4.

mixing bowl with the risen batter. Add cold water enough to thin the batter to where it will easily pour. Cook as directed above under "Early American Notes on Pancakes." *Note*: If very brown pancakes are desired, add 1 tablespoon sugar to the batter mixture.

GREAT-GRANDMOTHER MITCHELL'S OLD-FASHIONED FLANNEL CAKES

4 cups milk
3 tablespoons yeast[7]
1 teaspoon salt

Flour to suit
1 tablespoon butter, melted
2 eggs, well beaten

At night before retiring put the milk and yeast into a large wooden mixing bowl. Stir in the salt and enough flour to make a stiff batter. Beat the mixture thoroughly. Cover the bowl with a thick towel and set aside in a warm place until morning. The next morning whip in the melted butter and the frothy beaten eggs. Cook as directed above under "Early American Notes on Pancakes."

PRE-CIVIL WAR PLANTATION GRAHAM PANCAKES

3 egg yolks, well beaten
1 teaspoon salt
1 teaspoon baking soda, dissolved in hot water
3 cups sour milk
or
3 cups buttermilk

1/2 tablespoon butter, melted
2 cups graham flour
1 cup flour
3 egg whites, stiffly beaten

---

7. Recipes in *Natural Baking the Old Fashioned Way,* by the author.

Put the beaten custardlike egg yolks into a large wooden mixing bowl. Stir in the salt, baking soda, sour milk or buttermilk, and the melted butter. Then blend the graham flour with the regular flour. Alternately stir this and the fluffy beaten egg whites into the bowl until both are all used up. Cook as directed above under "Early American Notes on Pancakes," as soon as the batter is properly mixed. *Note:* Sweet milk may be substituted for the sour milk or buttermilk called for in this recipe. In such cases add 2 teaspoons cream of tartar to the batter.

MRS. ROSECRANS'S CORNMEAL FLAPJACKS

2 egg yolks, well beaten	2 tablespoons molasses
1 teaspoon salt	or
1 teaspoon baking soda,	2 tablespoons honey
dissolved in hot water	1 tablespoon butter, melted
4 cups sour milk	1/2 cup flour
or	2 egg whites, stiffly beaten
4 cups buttermilk	Cornmeal to suit

Put the beaten custardlike egg yolks into a large wooden mixing bowl. Stir in the salt, baking soda, sour milk or buttermilk, molasses or honey, and the melted butter. Then alternately stir in the flour and fluffy beaten egg whites until both are all used up. Thicken with enough cornmeal to make a batter a trifle thicker than that used for flannel cakes. Cook as directed above under "Early American Notes on Pancakes." *Note:* General Rosecrans's mother liked these best when she made them with buttermilk and honey. The general enjoyed them more when she made them with sour milk and molasses. Either way is a delightful, taste-pleasing experience for breakfast Her son, William Starke

Rosecrans (1819–98), ate these identical pancakes for breakfast all during his childhood. He later became an eminent Union general during the Civil War. This man defeated Bragg at Murfreesboro, Tennessee, on January 3, 1863. He later lost to Bragg in the battle of Chickamauga, Georgia, in September of that same year.

OLD-FASHIONED NEW ENGLAND WAFFLES

2 cups flour	4 tablespoons butter
4 teaspoons baking powder	melted
1/2 teaspoon salt	2 egg whites, stiffly
1 tablespoon sugar	beaten
1 1/2 cups milk	2 egg yolks, well
	beaten

Sift the flour, baking powder, salt, and sugar together in a large wooden mixing bowl. In a separate bowl blend the milk and custardlike beaten egg yolks. Then put this mixture into the dry ingredients in the first bowl and beat until smooth. Stir in the melted butter. Lastly fold in the fluffy beaten egg whites. Pour some of the batter on the center of a well-buttered waffle iron that has been heated for about 10 minutes, or until smoking hot. Cook until the steam discontinues to issue from the waffle iron. Serve hot with a syrup or some chopped fresh fruit sprinkled over the top.

EARLY BOSTON ORANGE SURPRISE WAFFLES

2 cups flour	1/2 cup orange juice
1/2 teaspoon salt	2 orange rinds, grated
1/3 cup sugar	6 tablespoons butter,

4 teaspoons baking powder
1 cup milk
3 egg yolks, well beaten

melted
3 egg whites, stiffly
beaten

Sift the flour, salt, sugar, and baking powder together in a large wooden mixing bowl. In a separate bowl blend the milk and custardlike beaten egg yolks. Pour this over the dry ingredients in the first bowl and beat until smooth. Stir in the orange juice. grated orange rind, and the melted butter. Lastly fold in the fluffy beaten egg whites. Pour some of the batter on the center of a well-buttered waffle iron that has been heated for about 10 minutes, or until smoking hot. Cook until the steam discontinues to issue from the waffle iron. Serve with powdered sugar sprinkled over the top, or with a combination of fresh orange slices and whipped cream. *Note*: My great-great-grandmother often added 1/4 cup cornmeal as a delightful variation to these orange waffles. Try it.

GREAT-GRANDMOTHER SHAW'S HOMEMADE CHOCOLATE WAFFLES

2 cups flour
3 teaspoons baking
    powder
1 teaspoon salt
3/4 cup sugar
1 1/2 cups milk
2 egg yolks, well beaten

2 squares unsweetened
    chocolate, melted
5 tablespoons butter,
    melted
1 teaspoon vanilla
2 egg whites, stiffly
    beaten

Sift the flour, baking powder, salt, and sugar together in a large wooden mixing bowl. In a separate bowl blend the milk and custardlike beaten egg yolks. Pour this over the dry ingredients in the first bowl and beat until smooth. Stir in the melted chocolate, melted butter, and vanilla. Lastly fold in the fluffy beaten egg whites. Pour some of the batter on the center of a well-buttered waffle iron that has been heated for about 10 minutes, or until smoking hot. Cook until the steam discontinues to issue from the waffle iron. These may be served as small cakes with powdered sugar sprinkled over the top, or with hard sauce[8] or foamy sauce.[9] *Note*: My Great-grandmother Shaw often added 1 cup chopped nuts to the batter, or scattered them over the top of the waffle batter after it was first poured on the waffle iron.

RICE AND CORNMEAL WAFFLES IN OLD CHARLESTON

1/2 cup flour	1 cup boiled rice, cold
1/2 cup cornmeal	1 tablespoon butter,
1 teaspoon salt	melted
1/2 teaspoon baking soda,	Milk to suit
dissolved in hot water	2 egg whites, stiffly
2 egg yolks, well beaten	beaten

Sift the flour, cornmeal, and salt together in a large wooden mixing bowl. In a separate bowl blend the baking soda and custardlike beaten egg yolks. Pour this over the dry ingredients in the first bowl and beat until smooth. Stir in the cold boiled rice, melted butter, and enough milk to make a soft batter. Beat hard until the mixture is smooth. Lastly fold in the fluffy beaten egg whites. Pour some of the batter on the center of a well-buttered waffle iron that has been heated for about 10 minutes, or until smoking hot. Cook until the steam discontinues to issue from the

---

8. Recipes in Chapter 4.
9. Recipes in Chapter 4.

waffle iron. Serve with maple syrup. *Note*: Be especially careful in buttering your waffle iron for these waffles. The rice has a tendency to stick and foul up the iron.

COLONIAL ERA RISEN DOUGHNUTS

2 cups butter, soft
3 1/2 cups sugar
4 cups milk
1 1/4 cups yeast[10]
Flour to suit
4 eggs, well beaten

1 teaspoon salt
1 tablespoon mace
or
1 tablespoon nutmeg
2 teaspoons cinnamon

Cream the butter and sugar in a large wooden mixing bowl. Blend in the milk and yeast. Stir in 6 cups flour. Blend well and then cover the bowl with a thick towel. Set aside in a warm place to rise overnight. In the morning stir in the frothy beaten eggs, salt, and spices. Add enough flour to make a stiff dough. Cover the bowl again and set aside in a warm place for 3 hours, or until the dough is light. Then put the dough on a floured board (or counter-top) and roll it out into a 1/2-inch-thick sheet. Cut out the doughnuts and fry them in boiling butter or oil. Take out when lightly browned. Sift powdered sugar over them while still hot.

GREAT-GREAT-GRANDMOTHER HORTON'S BEST QUICK DOUGHNUTS

1 cup butter, soft
2 cups sugar
4 eggs, well beaten
1 cup sour milk
or
1 cup sour cream

1 teaspoon baking soda, dissolved in hot water
1 teaspoon nutmeg
1/2 teaspoon cinnamon
Flour to suit

10. Recipes in *Natural Baking the Old Fashioned Way*, by the author.

Cream the butter and sugar in a large wooden mixing bowl. Blend in the frothy beaten eggs, sour milk *or* sour cream, baking soda, and spices. Add enough flour to make a pretty soft dough. Put the dough on a floured board (or countertop) and roll it out in a 1/2-inch-thick sheet. Or you may simply cut chunks of dough from the mass. If the dough is rolled out, cut the doughnuts to the size and shape desired. Fry them in boiling butter or oil. Take out when lightly browned. Sift powdered sugar over them while still hot.

MRS. CODY'S
DELIGHTFUL FRIED BREAKFAST CABBAGE

1 head cabbage, boiled	Pepper to taste
1 tablespoon butter, melted	4 tablespoons cream
Salt to taste	2 eggs, well beaten

Finely chop up the cold boiled cabbage. Drain it until very dry. Then stir in the melted butter, salt, pepper, cream, and frothy beaten eggs. Put into a buttered frying pan and slowly heat. Stir until the mixture becomes smoking hot. Then let it stand just long enough to brown slightly on the underside. Put a flat dish over the pan, upside down, and turn the fried cabbage out on it. Serve while hot. *Note*: This delicious early American breakfast dish was served to William Frederick Cody (1846–1917) long before he ever became so widely known as "Buffalo Bill." It was an old family recipe that was handed down for a great number of years.

16

Dainty Treats for the
Sick with Natural Foods

ARROWROOT JELLY IN THE COLONIES

2 teaspoons arrowroot, heaping
2 teaspoons sugar

1 cup water, boiling
1 teaspoon lemon juice

Wet the arrowroot in a little cold water and blend it to a smooth paste. Then stir the sugar into the boiling water until it dissolves. Bring to a boil and stir in the arrowroot paste. Continue stirring until clear, boiling steadily all the while, and blend in the lemon juice. Wet a cup in ice water. Pour the thickened jelly mixture from the pan and set it aside to cool. Eat when cold with a mixture of sugar and cream flavored with rosewater. *Note*: This was commonly used in the old days and was considered to be an excellent corrective to weak bowels. It is an invaluable preparation in cases where wine is forbidden.

COLONIAL-STYLE ARROWROOT WINE JELLY

2 teaspoons arrowroot, heaping	1 cup water, boiling
	1 tablespoon brandy
2 teaspoons sugar, heaping	3 tablespoons wine

Wet the arrowroot in a little cold water and blend it to a smooth paste. Then stir the sugar into the boiling water until it dissolves. Bring to a boil and stir in the arrowroot paste. Continue stirring until clear, boiling steadily all the while, and blend in the brandy and wine. Wet a cup in ice water. Pour the thickened jelly mixture from the pan and set aside to cool. Eat when cold with a mixture of sugar and cream flavored with rosewater. *Note:* This was commonly used in the old days and was considered to be an excellent corrective to weak bowels. It was better than the above and used more frequently.

GREAT-GREAT-GRANDMOTHER HORTON'S ARROWROOT BLANC MANGE

1 1/2 tablespoons arrowroot	1 cup milk, boiling
	Vanilla or other extract to suit taste
2 teaspoons sugar	

Wet the arrowroot in a little cold water and blend it to a smooth paste. Then stir the sugar into the boiling milk until it dissolves. Bring to a boil and stir in the arrowroot paste. Continue stirring until it thickens well, boiling steadily all the while and blend in the vanilla. Wet a cup in ice water. Pour the thickened jelly mixture from the pan and set it aside to cool. Eat when cold with a mixture of sugar and cream flavored with rosewater.

EARLY AMERICAN INDIAN MEAL GRUEL

| 1 cup Indian meal | 8 cups water, boiling |
| 1 tablespoon flour | Salt to taste |

Blend the Indian meal and flour. Wet with a little cold water and beat it to a smooth paste. Stir this into the water while it is actually boiling hard. Then let it simmer for 1/2 hour while stirring up well from the bottom of the pan. Pour into a warmed bowl and season to taste with salt. Eat while warm with cream. *Note*: Many old-timers liked this gruel better if it was sweetened and then flavored with nutmeg. But my Great-great-grandmother Horton liked it better with a little pepper added to the salt. If a laxative was desired she omitted the wheat flour altogether. And she recommended not using any cream on it while eating.

MILK AND RICE GRUEL ON THE PLANTATION

3 tablespoons rice, ground	Pinch of salt
4 cups milk, boiling	Sugar to suit
	Nutmeg to suit

Put the ground rice in a little cold milk and blend it to a smooth paste. Stir the rice paste and salt into the pan of boiling milk. Let it boil together for 10 minutes while stirring continuously. Pour the gruel into a warmed bowl. Flavor to taste with sugar and nutmeg. Eat while warm with cream. *Note*: Some old-timers substituted Indian meal in place of the rice, which was considered to be an astringent. In this case the mixture should be simmered for 1/2 hour before serving.

THE FARRAGUTS' SPECIAL SAGO GRUEL

2 tablespoons sago
2 cups water, cold
3 teaspoons sugar
1/4 cup wine

1 tablespoon lemon juice
Nutmeg to taste
Pinch of salt

Put the sago into a saucepan with the cold water. Heat by setting the saucepan in a larger pan of boiling water. Stir often and let it simmer for 1 hour. Then boil for 10 minutes while stirring continuously. Add the sugar, wine, lemon juice, nutmeg, and salt. Pour into a bowl to cool and set. Eat warm, if preferred, with cream poured over it. *Note*: In Mrs. Farragut's day, it was recommended that "the wine and nutmeg should be omitted if the patient is feverish." This was an old family favorite used by the mother of David Glasgow Farragut (1801–1870), the first admiral of the United States Navy. He took the Confederate cities of New Orleans in 1862 and Mobile in 1864 as a Union naval officer.

BEST OLD-TIME FLAXSEED LEMONADE

4 tablespoons flax-
  seed, whole
4 cups water, boiling

Juice of 3 lemons
Sugar to taste

Put the flaxseed into a pitcher and pour the boiling water over them. Cover the pitcher and let it steep for 3 hours. Then blend in the lemon juice and sugar. If the lemonade is too thick, add cold water enough to thin sufficiently. Set on ice to chill before drinking. *Note*: In great grandmother's day this drink was said to be exceptionally good for helping cure colds.

GREAT-GRANDMOTHER SHAW'S TAPIOCA JELLY

3 cups water, cold
1 cup tapioca
Sugar to taste

Juice of 1 lemon
Pinch of lemon peel,
grated

Put the cold water into a small saucepan. Soak the tapioca in the water for 4 hours. Then set the pan in a larger pan of boiling water. Pour more lukewarm water over the tapioca if it has absorbed too much of the liquid. Heat slowly while stirring frequently. If too thick after it begins to clear, add a very little boiling water. When quite clear, blend in the sugar, lemon juice, and grated peel. Pour into molds or cups and set aside to cool. Eat when cold with a mixture of sugar and cream. Flavor this with almond extract or rosewater if desired.

OLD NEW ORLEANS FLUFFY BOILED RICE

1/2 cup whole rice
1 cup milk

Pinch of salt
1 egg, well beaten

Put the rice into a saucepan with just enough water to cover it. Bring to a boil. When the rice is nearly done, pour off the water. Stir in the milk and heat it slowly. Let it simmer—taking care it does not scorch—until the milk boils up well. Stir in the salt and then whip in the frothy beaten egg. Pour into a warmed bowl and eat while hot with cream, sugar, and nutmeg. *Note*: This was an old favorite on many plantations as well as in the kitchens of the finest homes.

ORIGINAL COLONIAL PERIOD APPLE WATER

1 large juicy apple   4 cups water, cold

Pare and quarter the apple, but do not core it. Put it on the stove in a porcelain saucepan with the water. Closely cover and bring to a boil. Cook until the apple stews to pieces. Strain the liquor through a coarse muslin cloth. Press the apple hard in the cloth. Strain this again through a finer cloth. Then set the juice aside to cool. Sweeten if necessary, to individual taste. Chill before drinking. *Note*: This is both a refreshing and palatable old-fashioned beverage.

GREAT-GREAT-GRANDMOTHER DANIELS'S HOMEMADE PANADA

6 crackers, split	Nutmeg to suit
2 tablespoons sugar	Boiling water to suit
Salt to suit	

Pile the split crackers in a bowl in layers. Scatter the sugar, salt, and nutmeg among them. Cover the crackers with boiling water. Put a tight lid on the bowl and set aside in a warm place for 1 hour. The crackers should be almost clear and soft as jelly, but not broken. Eat from the bowl, with more sugar sprinkled on the crackers if desired. If properly made, this old-fashioned panada is difficult to beat.

EARLY SOUTHERN MILK TOAST FOR INVALIDS

Pare the crusts from some slices of stale bread. Toast each slice nicely. Then dip the slices, as they are toasted and still hot, in boiling water. Butter each slice, salt slightly and lay in a deep covered dish. Meanwhile pour enough milk into a saucepan to cover the bread slices in the bowl. Quickly bring it to a boil, salt it slightly, and melt in bits of butter. Pour this over the toast. Cover the dish closely and let it stand for 5 minutes. Then serve while steaming hot. *Note*: This milk toast is best when made with stale homemade wheat and Indian bread[1] or whole wheat bread.[2] In the estimation of my great-great-grandmother it was a delightful dish for a family tea as well as for serving to invalids.

GREAT-GREAT-GRANDMOTHER NORTHRUP'S BREAD PANADA

Pare the crusts from some slices of stale bread and toast the slices nicely. Do not burn or scorch the slices. Pile the slices in a bowl in layers. Sprinkle each layer lightly with sugar and a little salt. Cover well with boiling water. Cover the bowl tightly and set it in a pan of boiling water. Simmer gently until the contents of the bowl are like jelly. Eat this panada from the bowl while it is warm. Sprinkle powdered sugar and nutmeg over the top. *Note*: Some housewives of yesteryear called this a "bread jelly."

OLDEN DAY PLANTATION WHEATEN GRITS

4 tablespoons grits (cracked wheat)	1 cup milk, hot
	Pinch of salt
4 cups water, boiling	Sugar to taste

Put the grits into a large kettle and add enough cold water to wet well. Set aside to soak for 1 full hour. Then add the boiling water and let it simmer for 1 hour. Stir often to prevent burning. Then add the milk and salt. Simmer for 1/2

---

1. Recipes in *Natural Baking the Old Fashioned Way*, by the author.
2. Ibid.

hour longer. Sweeten to taste. *Note*: This recipe was popular in the Old South as a mild laxative, especially good when the milk was omitted. Even in those days people were conscious of, and concerned with, the inherent evils of drugs and some types of patent medicines. My own Great-great-grandmother Horton once said, "When it can be done without drugs, it is far better."

GREAT-GRANDMOTHER MITCHELL'S ARROWROOT CUSTARD

3 teaspoons arrowroot, heaping	2 tablespoons sugar
	2 cups milk, boiling
1 egg	Vanilla to suit

Put the arrowroot with a little cold water and blend it to a smooth paste. Put the egg into a wooden mixing bowl and beat in the sugar. Continue beating hard until the mixture is light and frothy. Then stir the arrowroot paste into the boiling milk. Stir for 3 minutes and immediately remove from the stove. Whip the frothy beaten egg into this and put it back on the stove. Simmer for 2 minutes longer. Flavor with vanilla to suit taste. Pour into molds or cups and set aside to cool. It may be eaten while warm if preferred.

COLONIAL ERA UNLEAVENED WAFERS OR BISCUITS

Mix any good, dry flour to a stiff dough with milk and salt. Put the dough on a floured board (or countertop) and roll it out into a 1/8-inch-thick sheet. Cut into round cakes and roll these again almost as thin as paper. Bake in a very quick oven (450 degrees). *Note*: These wafers may also be mixed with water instead of milk. They are simple to make and extremely palatable. And they go well with all kinds of soups and broths.

UNRIVALED HOMEMADE
EARLY AMERICAN MILK PORRIDGE

1 tablespoon Indian meal	Pinch of salt
1 cup flour	2 cups milk
2 cups water, boiling	

Blend the Indian meal and flour in a wooden mixing bowl. Wet it with a little cold water and beat it to a smooth paste. Stir this into the boiling water and let it simmer for 20 minutes. Stir continuously. Then add the salt and milk. Bring to a quick boil and then let it simmer for 10 minutes longer. Stir often as this mixture cooks. Serve while hot, with sugar and milk or cream stirred into it.

MRS. HAMLIN'S TAPIOCA BLANC MANGE

1 cup tapioca	Rosewater to suit
2 cups water, cold	or
3 cups milk, boiling	Vanilla to suit
3 tablespoons sugar	

Soak the tapioca in the cold water for 4 hours. Then stir this mixture into a saucepan with the boiling milk. Add the sugar and let it slowly simmer for 15 minutes. Stir continuously as it cooks. Remove from the stove and flavor to taste with the rosewater or vanilla. Pour into molds or cups and set aside to cool. Eat when cold with plain cream. It may also be eaten warm if desired. *Note*: This is the way in which Mrs. Hamlin fed it to her son, Hannibal, whenever he was feeling ill. He preferred it with the rosewater, but she liked it better made with vanilla as a flavoring. It was a popular preparation in their household. And who was Hannibal Hamlin? He turned out to be Lincoln's vice-president in 1860.

Appendix 1
Unique Natural Food Menu Suggestions

Vegetarian or meatless menu planning is easy. The most important factor involved, of course, is the nutritiousness of the food served. Equally as important is the food's digestibility. And, lastly, the food's palatability. Harmony in food offerings is the key to appetizing meals. The food flavors, colors, and odors should always complement one another. The following menu ideas will be of great assistance as a basis for planning delightful meatless meals in the home. The variation is unlimited—if a little imagination is utilized. Recipes for every food item suggested in these menus are included in the various chapters of this book.

Corn Soup

Mushroom Pork Chops

Baked Pumpkin   Succotash

Hot Slaw

Cherry Pie

Tomato Soup

Stuffed Cabbage

Buttered Parsnips   Boiled Sea-kale

Celery Salad

Currant-Raspberry Tarts

Vegetable Soup

Cheese-Bran Loaf

Baked Hominy   Mashed Turnips

Raw Tomato Salad

Pumpkin Custard

Hulled Corn Soup
Baked Omelet
Pea Fritters   Baked Onions
Favorite Tomato Salad
Date Pudding

Cream of Celery Soup
Nutty Baked Vegetable Casserole
Fried Eggplant   Buttered Artichokes
Summer Salad
Coconut Pie

Green Pea Soup
Tomato with Scrambled Eggs
Parsnip Fritters   Fried Tomatoes
Cranberry-Vegetable Salad
Cranberry Pudding

Raspberry Royal
Green Pepper Casserole
Broccoli and Eggs   Green Peas
Cheese Salad
Fresh Coconut Pudding

Pea-Tomato Soup
Peanut Butter-Rice Steaks
Stewed Beets   Stewed Cauliflower
Cucumber Salad
Fresh Peach Pie

Mock Bisque Soup
Baked Peanut Steak Patties
Buttered Okra   Mashed Parsnips
Waldorf Salad
Strawberry Pie

Strawberry Sherbet
Stuffed Baked Tomatoes
Hominy Croquettes   Ladies' Cabbage
Hot Cabbage Salad
Bread Pudding

Julienne Soup
Stuffed Baked Eggplant
Potato Croquettes   Stewed Cucumbers
Potato Salad
Pumpkin Custard

Cranberry Juice Cocktail
Cheese Souffle
Fried Parsnips   Roast Sweet Potatoes
Cold Slaw
Fresh Coconut Pudding

Creamed Tomato Drink

Green Corn Pudding

Scalloped Cauliflower   Spinach à la Crême

Lettuce Salad

Creamy Rice Pudding

Black Bean Soup

Bean Loaf

Potato Puffs   Boiled Beets

Cold Cabbage Salad

Cranberry Tart

Creamed Pea Soup

Asparagus in Ambush

Fried Cucumbers   Sauerkraut

Cucumbers-Olives-Celery-Onions

Coconut Pie

Bread Soup

Nutty Cheese Loaf

Rice Croquettes   Green Corn Fritters

Macedoine Salad

Bread Pudding

Appendix 2
Table of Natural Ingredients

A Note on Natural Ingredients

Each ingredient called for in these healthful old-time recipes is listed in its most commonly used form for convenience of understanding. Nevertheless, every ingredient should be pure, chemical free, and without unnatural preservatives. Every item is relatively easy to procure. Many can now be obtained in regular supermarkets—often in a special section reserved for natural foods. Others are readily found in any good health food or natural food store. They are also available through mail-order outlets. An excellent guide to natural food sources is available for $1.00 from: Rodale Press, 33 East Minor Street, Emmaus, Pa. 18049

Commercial Item	Natural Counterpart
Baking powder	Use only those brands containing no aluminum compounds. *or* Substitute 2 egg whites for every teaspoon of baking powder called for.
Baking soda	Many people prefer using baking powder instead. Baking soda is generally avoided because it is believed to destroy B vitamins in other foods. If baking powder is substituted use 2 teaspoons for every 1/2 teaspoon baking soda. *or* Substitute 1 or 2 tablespoons yeast.
Brown sugar	Natural brown sugar or honey.
Butter	Raw or natural butter. Some people prefer natural margarine over any kind of butter. *See Margarine.*
Cheese	Natural cheese made from raw milk. Cheese without chemical additives. Cheese not labeled "processed."
Chocolate	Pure chocolate or substitute carob powder. Carob is wholesome and readily digested. It is richer than chocolate in protein and lower in starch and fat. Carob is stronger flavored. Use less when substituting in recipes.

Coconut	Unsweetened coconut, freshly grated.
Cooking oil[1]	Any nonhydrogenated liquid vegetable oils. Cold pressed oils are higher in essential fatty acids. They are free of all preservatives. Try: cold pressed corn oil, cold pressed olive oil, cold pressed sesame oil, cold pressed soy oil, pure safflower oil (an all purpose oil).
Cornmeal (degermed)[2]	Coarse ground cornmeal or whole corn kernels. Can be ground at home. Contains the germ of the kernel.
Corn starch	Arrowroot starch is preferred.
Cottage cheese	Natural cottage cheese.
Eggs[3]	Eggs produced by laying hens raised with a rooster. Such eggs are called "fertile" and contain important enzymes as well as hormones.
Flour[4] (also called *wheat flour*)	Unbleached flour. Contains no foreign preservatives or bleaches. Has not been chemically treated in any manner. Note: Seal in plastic bags or jars to preserve its freshness. Can also be frozen.

1. Preservatives are usually added to prevent rancidity.
2. Refined to a point where it has little nutritional value. Made from sterile hybrid corn.
3. Eggs are usually sprayed with disinfectant.
4. Overrefined wheat product. Contains chemical bleaches.

Fruit	Organic fruits or those organically grown. Fruit grown without chemical fertilizers or sprays. Use fresh fruit or pure home-canned varieties.
Honey	Unfiltered, unblended, uncooked honey. It has more minerals and enzymes.
Macaroni and spaghetti[5]	Soy macaroni and spaghetti. Unbleached wheat macaroni and spaghetti. Sesame macaroni and spaghetti.
Margarine	Natural margarine. Any good margarine made without chemical additives. One of the best is made from soybean extracts. Some people like to use corn germ oil as a substitute in recipes.
Milk[6]	Raw milk, preferably from certified dairy herds. If unavailable, fortify regular milk with powdered milk.
Molasses	Unsulphured molasses. Blackstrap molasses is one of the best to use. It contains valuable minerals and B vitamins. Has a strong flavor.
Oats	Old-fashioned rolled oats, unhulled oats, oat groats or steel-cut oats. Never use commercially processed oatmeal. Rolled oats are simply the flattened whole oat kernels.

5. Commercial products made with bleached flour and often contain chemical preservatives.

6. Pasteurized milk has reduced calcium. Enzymes and hormones are destroyed in processing. Preservatives are often added to the milk.

Peanut butter	Nonhydrogenated peanut butter.
Rice	Natural brown rice tastes better and it is much more nutritional. Wild rice, or as a final choice, "converted" rice.
Salad oil	*See Cooking oil.*
Salt	Sea salt or unrefined salt. Contains important trace elements lacking in most diets. Sea salt does not contain chemicals as does ordinary table salt.
Shortening[7]	Pure safflower oil shortening.
Spices and herbs	Use commercial dried herbs and spices. They are generally pure. Fresh herbs may be home grown in a garden or pots.
Starch	Arrowroot starch is generally preferred over cornstarch.
Sugar	Natural or raw sugar. Honey is often substituted for sugar in a recipe. If it is, use only 2/3 the amount of sugar called for.
Vanilla or other flavorings	Use only extracts. All extracts must be pure according to federal law.
Vegetables[8]	Organic vegetables or those organically grown. Vegetables grown without chemical fertilizers or sprays. Use fresh vegetables or pure home-canned varieties.
Wheat flour	*See Flour.*

---

7. Often contains chemical additives. Carefully check label.

8. Frozen or canned commercial vegetables contain chemical preservatives or other unsavory additives.

Index